Compelling Essays On AI And Law

Advanced Series On Artificial Intelligence (AI) And Law

Dr. Lance B. Eliot, MBA, PhD

ISBN: 978-1-73-630313-9

DEDICATION

To my incredible daughter, Lauren, and my incredible son, Michael.

Forest fortuna adiuvat (from the Latin; good fortune favors the brave).

CONTENTS

Acknowledgments iii

Chapters

1 Introduction to AI and Law 1

2 AI & Law: Echo Chambers In The Law 21

3 AI & Law: Role Reversible Judgment 27

4 AI & Law: When AI Is The Criminal 33

5 AI & Law: Apologetic AI Legal Troubles 39

6 AI & Law: Personal Digital Identity 45

7 AI & Law: Stockpiling Legal Postures 51

8 AI & Law: Law As Code 57

9 AI & Law: Lawyers As Coders 63

10 AI & Law: Agile AI And Law 69

11 AI & Law: Legal Advice By Nanosecond 75

12 AI & Law: AI-Based Co-Counsel 81

13 AI & Law: Deferential Behaviors In Law 87

14 AI & Law: Slowing AI Wheels Of Justice 93

15 AI & Law: Dehumanizing Lawyers 99

16 AI & Law: Gifting Of AI Legal Advice 105

17 AI & Law: When AI Is Evidentiary 111

18 AI & Law: Legal Maps 117

19 AI & Law: Posthumanization 123

20 AI & Law: AI Law Not Computable 129

21 AI & Law: Collective Intelligence 135

22 AI & Law: Limits Of Human Mind 141

23 AI & Law: Judicial Machine Readability 147

24 AI & Law: Legal Ecosystem 153

25 AI & Law: Oxford – Autonomous Levels 159

Appendix A: Teaching with this Material & Bibliography...... 163

Appendix B: Supplemental Figures and Charts 173

About the Author 205

Note: Visuals are collected together in Appendix B, rather than being interjected into the chapter contents, for ease of reading, enhanced flow, and to see the visuals altogether.

Dr. Lance B. Eliot

ACKNOWLEDGMENTS

I have been the beneficiary of advice and counsel by many friends, colleagues, family, investors, and many others. I want to thank everyone that has aided me throughout my career. I write from the heart and the head, having experienced first-hand what it means to have others around you that support you during the good times and the tough times.

To renowned scholar and colleague, Dr. Warren Bennis, I offer my deepest thanks and appreciation, especially for his calm and insightful wisdom and support.

To billionaire and university trustee, Mark Stevens and his generous efforts toward funding and supporting the Stevens Center for Innovation.

To Peter Drucker, William Wang, Aaron Levie, Peter Kim, Jon Kraft, Cindy Crawford, Jenny Ming, Steve Milligan, Chis Underwood, Frank Gehry, Buzz Aldrin, Steve Forbes, Bill Thompson, Dave Dillon, Alan Fuerstman, Larry Ellison, Jim Sinegal, John Sperling, Mark Stevenson, Anand Nallathambi, Thomas Barrack, Jr., and many other innovators and leaders that I have met and gained mightily from doing so.

Thanks to Ed Trainor, Kevin Anderson, James Hickey, Wendell Jones, Ken Harris, DuWayne Peterson, Mike Brown, Jim Thornton, Abhi Beniwal, Al Biland, John Nomura, Eliot Weinman, John Desmond, and many others for their unwavering support during my career.

Thanks goes to the Stanford University CodeX Center for Legal Informatics and the Stanford University Computer Science department for their generous support, and for the insightfual and inspirational discussions and feedback from my many fellow colleagues there.

And most of all thanks as always to Lauren and Michael, for their ongoing support and for having seen me writing and heard much of this material during the many months involved in writing it. To their patience and willingness to listen.

Dr. Lance B. Eliot

CHAPTER 1

INTRODUCTION TO
AI AND LAW

This book provides a series of compelling essays encompassing the burgeoning field of AI and the law. These essays are ostensibly standalone and do not require any prior familiarity with the AI and law topic. You are welcome to read the essays in whichever order you might prefer. The essays have been numbered and sequenced as chapters for ease of referring to the discussions and not due to any need to read one before another.

The essays provide a helpful overview and entry point into the field of AI and law. You will find the essays relatively easy to read and eschew arcane techno-terminology, aiming to layout the vital aspects in clear language and seeking to be readily grasped. The chosen topics entail the latest and hottest trends in the AI and law arena.

For those of you that are potentially interested in knowing more about AI and the law in a deeper way, you might consider my other books on this subject:

- *"AI and Legal Reasoning Essentials"* by Dr. Lance Eliot

- *"Artificial Intelligence and LegalTech Essentials"* by Dr. Lance Eliot

- *"Decisive Essays on AI and Law"* by Dr. Lance Eliot

- *"Ingenious Essays on AI and Law"* by Dr. Lance Eliot

- *"Incisive Research on AI and Law"* by Dr. Lance Eliot

The first two books are more akin to textbook-style orientations to the AI and the law field.

The other books are a further collection of my essays and the latter book contains my in-depth research papers (oriented toward legal and AI scholars). The books are available on Amazon and at major bookseller sites.

One of the most frequent questions that I get asked during my webinars, seminars, and university courses about AI and the law consists of what the phrase "AI and the law" actually refers to.

That's a fair question and deserves a useful answer. In a moment, I will borrow from my other books to provide an explanation about the meaning of "AI and the law" and then dovetail into a brief indication about each of the essays contained in this collection.

Per the essays, you'll end up seeing that there is a great deal of enthusiastic spirit for AI and the law, and likewise a sizable dollop of angst and trepidation about the intertwining of the two. In my view, whether you love it or hate it, there is no stopping the steamroller moving ahead that is going to infuse AI together with the law.

I would urge that any lawyer worth their salt ought to be learning about AI and the law. This will assuredly be especially important for those that are just now starting their legal careers, which I mention because the odds are that the convergence of AI and the law will have an especially pronounced effect throughout your lifelong legal efforts.

For those of you that might be going a more so academic route in the legal realm, rather than being a practitioner of the law per se, the beauty of AI and the law is that there is ample room for new research and a grand opportunity to make a demonstrative mark on the field. There are numerous open questions and plenty of challenges that provide abundant possibility for making a decided mark on this still nascent field of study.

Despite the fact that the field of AI and the law has been studied for many years, dating back to the beginning of the AI field itself, please be aware that we have only scratched the surface on this interweaving. Anyone with a desire to push the boundaries of these two realms will readily find plenty of rampways to do so.

If you are curious about the possible research avenues to pursue, make sure to take a look at my book on *AI and Legal Reasoning Essentials* since it provides a solid foundation on the research to-date and postulates what might be coming down the pike in future research activities, and then consider my book on *Incisive Research on AI and Law*. I bid you welcome to the field and wish you the best of luck in your endeavors.

I next provide a brief introduction to the field of AI and law, which echoes my thoughts as variously expressed in my other books and my various articles and postings.

AI And Law

In my viewpoint, Artificial Intelligence (AI) and the field of law are synergistic partners. The intertwining of AI and Law can generally be categorized into two major approaches:

- **AI as applied to Law**
- **Law as applied to AI**

Let us consider each of those two approaches.

AI As Applied To Law

AI as applied to law consists of trying to utilize AI technologies and AI techniques for the embodiment of law, potentially being able to perform legal tasks and undertake legal reasoning associated with the practice of law. Those scholars, experts, and practitioners that have this focus are using AI to aid or integrate artificial intelligence into how humans practice law, either augmenting lawyers and other legal professionals or possibly replacing them in the performance of various legal tasks.

Crafting such AI is especially hard to accomplish, problematic in many ways, and there have been and continue to emerge a myriad of attempts to achieve this difficult goal or aspiration.

The rise of LegalTech and LawTech, which is modern digital technology used to support and enable lawyers, law offices, and the like throughout the practice of law are gradually and inexorably being bolstered by the addition of AI capabilities.

There are many indications already of this trend rapidly expanding in the existing and growing LegalTech and LawTech marketplace. Notably, the potent AI and LegalTech/LawTech combination has been drawing the rapt attention of Venture Capitalists (VCs). According to figures by the National Venture Capital Association (NVCA), the last several years have witnessed VC's making key investments of over one billion dollars towards law-related tech startups, many of which have some form of an AI capability involved.

Most of the AI developed so far for LegalTech and LawTech is only able to assist lawyers and legal professions in rather modest and simplistic ways. For example, AI might speed-up the search for documents during e-discovery or might enhance the preparation of a contract by identifying pertinent contractual language from a corpus of prior contracts.

Where the field of applying AI to law is seeking to head involves having AI that can perform legal-minded tasks that human lawyers and other legal professionals perform. In essence, creating AI systems that can undertake legal reasoning. This is commonly referred to as AI for Legal Reasoning (AILR).

In a sense, legal reasoning goes to the core of performing legal tasks and is considered the ultimate pinnacle as it were for the efforts to try and apply AI to law. It is undoubtedly one of the most exciting areas of the AI-applied-to-law arena and one that holds both tremendous promise and perhaps some angst and possible somber qualms.

Law As Applied To AI

The other major approach that combines AI and law focuses on the law as applied AI. This is an equally crucial perspective on the AI and law topic.

Sometimes this is also referred to as the **Governance of AI**, though there are those that believe that to be a somewhat narrower perspective on the topic. In any case, the focus is primarily on the governance of AI and how our laws might need to be revised, updated, or revamped in light of AI systems.

You likely already know that AI is experiencing quite a resurgence and has become a key focus of the tech field, along with gaining attention throughout society. AI is being rapidly infused into a wide variety of industries and domain specialties, including AI in the financial sector, AI in the medical domain, and so on.

This rapid pace of AI adoption has opened the eyes of society about the benefits of AI but also has gradually brought to the forefront many of the costs or negative aspects that AI can bring forth. Some assert that our existing laws are insufficient to cope with the advances that AI is producing. Thus, the need to closely examine our existing laws and possibly revamp them for an era and future of ubiquitous AI.

Expected Impacts

Let's consider how AI and the law can impact those in the AI field, and also contemplate how it can impact those in the field of law.

If you are an AI specialist, you should certainly be interested in the AI and law topic, either due to the possibilities of advancing AI by discovering how to leverage AI into the legal domain or due to the potential of how existing and future laws are going to impact the exploration and fielding of AI systems.

If you are a lawyer or legal specialist, you ought to be interested in the AI and law topic too, for the same reasons as the AI specialist, though perhaps with some added stake in the game.

What is the added stake?

If AI can ultimately become advanced enough to practice law, there is concern by some that it could potentially replace the need for human lawyers and other human legal-related law practitioners.

Some liken this to the famous and telling remark about commitment as exhibited via a chicken and a pig. A chicken and a pig are walking along and discussing what they might do together, and the chicken offers that perhaps they ought to open a restaurant that serves ham-n-eggs. Upon a moment of reflection, the pig speaks up and says that if they did so, the chicken would only be involved (making the eggs), while the pig would end-up being fully committed (being the bacon).

In that sense, AI specialists in this topic are involved, while legal specialists and lawyers are committed. Meanwhile, for those of you squarely in the field of law, lest you think that AI specialists are to be spared the same fate of being overtaken by AI, you will be perhaps surprised to know that there are efforts underway to craft AI that makes AI, such as in the field of Machine Learning (ML), a specialty known as AutoML, which could potentially put human developers of AI out of a job. What is good for the goose is good for the gander. Or, it might be that what is bad for the goose is equally bad for the gander.

About These Essays

Now that you've gotten an initial synopsis regarding the topic of AI and law, let's take a moment to briefly take a look at the essays assembled for this decisive collection.

Chapter 1 – Introduction To AI And Law

Key briefing points about this chapter:

- This book is a collection of crucial essays about AI and the law

- The essays are provided as numbered chapters (the sequence is not essential)

- AI and the law consist of two key facets

- One facet is AI as applied to the law (a mainstay of this collection)

- The other facet is applying the law to AI (i.e., governance of AI)

Chapter 2 - AI & Law: Echo Chambers In The Law

Key briefing points about this chapter:

- It is common to refer to those that hear and see the same thing to be in an echo chamber

- There is a squelching of other ideas that takes place, purposely or by happenstance

- At times there are attorneys in say a law firm that can get themselves into an echo chamber

- Echo chambers have some benefits but also can be at the cost of new ideas

- The advent of AI-based legal reasoning could be an interloper to disrupt such echoes

Chapter 3 - AI & Law: Role Reversible Judgment

Key briefing points about this chapter:

- AI is increasingly being infused into the practice of law

- A great deal of debate centers on whether AI will be suitable in the role of judges

- One argument is that AI won't have a first-person perspective and only third-person

- Without the capacity to walk in the shoes of another there is concern over AI judgments

- Counterarguments include AI as judicial neutrality, plus AI embodiment of sentimentality

Chapter 4 - AI & Law: When AI Is The Criminal

Key briefing points about this chapter:

- There is eagerness in using AI for the betterment of humanity

- Though not as apparent is the use of AI for committing criminal acts

- If a human crook employs AI for illegal efforts there is still a human responsible

- Not so clearcut is what to do when the AI morphs from good to bad and commits crimes

- Some wonder whether existing laws will be able to contend with AI as the crook

Chapter 5 - AI & Law: Apologetic AI Legal Troubles

Key briefing points about this chapter:

- AI systems are increasingly being programmed to emit apologies

- Some like the apology and feel better, while others find it insulting and a hollow gesture

- There is a substantial body of legal literature on the topic of law-and-apologies

- In some respects, an apology is legally exculpatory and in other ways legally inculpatory

- Firms making AI might be digging themselves a hole, plus AI liability could later arise

Chapter 6 - AI & Law: Personal Digital Identity

Key briefing points about this chapter:

- A recent class session of the MIT Computational Law 2021 course discussed digital identity

- Included were Wyoming State Senator Chris Rothfuss and personal digital identity legislation

- The approach reflects the legal notion of personal digital identity as a bundled agency

- In addition to sorely needed legal imbuements, the role of AI-based enablement can add value

- Envision a layer of self-governing digital identity being run by an AI system on your behalf

Chapter 7 - AI & Law: Stockpiling Legal Postures

Key briefing points about this chapter:

- Lawyers create legal arguments and must do so with moves and countermoves in mind

- AI-based legal reasoning systems will gradually augment those laborious efforts

- Imagine the AI as a kind-of chess-playing capability though in the realm of legal arguments

- You could potentially have the AI generate a slew of newly minted legal arguments

- If so, should they be made open to all or can you keep them a secret (an ethical dilemma)

Chapter 8 - AI & Law: Law As Code

Key briefing points about this chapter:

- There is a great deal of effort aiming toward "law as code" (it is headline-making)

- The gist is to somehow convert laws into programming code, allowing for digital usage

- This is much more than simply textual aspects and requires runnable capacities too

- A tremendous stumbling block is the inherent semantic indeterminism of the law

- Suggestions that we change our laws to be amenable to coding are brazen and unlikely

Chapter 9 – AI & Law: Lawyers As Coders

Key briefing points about this chapter:

- There is tremendous interest (and rancor) about the proposition of lawyers-as-coders

- Some assert that the future of the law and especially via AI will radically impact attorneys

- As such the argument exists that lawyers would be prudent to learn about coding

- Counterarguments are that lawyers should stick with their knitting and let coders code

- A recent webinar by Northwestern University is used herein to explore these tradeoffs

Chapter 10 - AI & Law: Agile AI And Law

Key briefing points about this chapter:

- Recent efforts to speed-up AI development are being coined as using Agile AI techniques

- Software development has historically relied upon the waterfall model of development

- In the classic waterfall, each step or stage is done one at a time, possibly elongating the process

- Agile AI leverages modern agile-based development involving sprints, scrums, etc.

- The use of Agile AI for developing AI-based or AI-infused LegalTech apps is being encouraged

Chapter 11 - AI & Law: Legal Advice By Nanosecond

Key briefing points about this chapter:

- Lawyers tend to charge for legal advice based on hourly work (or fractions thereof)

- ABA stipulations indicate that those lawyering fees are to abide by "reasonableness" factors

- The future of lawyering will encompass AI-based legal reasoning systems

- Those AI systems will run based on nanoseconds (one billionth of a second)

- How will lawyerly legal advice be charged when AI can do so on such fractions of time

Chapter 12 - AI & Law: AI-Based Co-Counsel

Key briefing points about this chapter:

- It is quite common that a client might need multiple lawyers covering particular specialties

- There are rules of conduct expected of such multi-lawyering arrangements

- The future is likely to consist of AI-based legal reasoning systems that can act as a lawyer

- Those AI systems are unlikely to be a monolith and more likely to be specialized

- Thus there are important questions about the interoperability of AI-to-AI multi-lawyering

Chapter 13 – AI & Law: Deferential Behaviors In Law

Key briefing points about this chapter:

- A recent study suggests that there are adverse outcomes in courts due to deferential behavior

- Besides individual differences, there are suggested patterns across societal segments

- Many assume that AI might inevitably overcome such aspects

- It is presumed that AI-based legal reasoning systems would be unbiased and neutral

- Recent aspects about today's AI showcase inherent biases and troubling aspects that can arise

Chapter 14 – AI & Law: Slowing AI Wheels Of Justice

Key briefing points about this chapter:

- We take at face value that going faster and faster is inherently sensible and productive

- Lawyers are continually pressured to get their legal work done soonest possible

- The advent of AI-based legal reasoning systems are bound to aid that speed/time quest

- Some though question whether the speeding up of the wheels of justice is sensible

- Perhaps those AI systems will need to be slowed down to match the humanity of the law

Chapter 15 - AI & Law: Dehumanizing Lawyers

Key briefing points about this chapter:

- There are a lot of jokes about lawyers and for which oftentimes are quite over-the-top

- And yet people tend to relish and respect an attorney once they have a personal need for one

- The advent of AI-based legal reasoning systems could shake-up the perception of attorneys

- One expressed qualm is that AI will lead to human lawyers being treated as though automata

- Dehumanizing of attorneys and the legal profession could be a sour outcome accordingly

Chapter 16 – AI & Law: Gifting Of AI Legal Advice

Key briefing points about this chapter:

- AI-based legal reasoning systems will arise as initially being semi-autonomous

- Gradually, there will be advancement toward fully autonomous versions

- It is widely assumed that such AI will be very expensive to use

- Can a law firm "gift" to the courts the use of an AI system to aid justice?

- Per an extendable interpretation of the Code of Judicial Ethics, the answer seems to be no

Chapter 17 - AI & Law: When AI Is Evidentiary

Key briefing points about this chapter:

- AI and Machine Learning (ML) systems are increasingly being used throughout society

- An open-ended issue surrounds the evidentiary nature of AI and ML

- Legal scholars are in the midst of debating the admissibility aspects

- One expressed viewpoint has compared AI/ML to the famous Daubert Criteria

- In brief, these authors contend that arguments can be made for and against such admissibility

Chapter 18 - AI & Law: Legal Maps

Key briefing points about this chapter:

- There are plenty of map apps and online maps available these days

- Using an electronic-based map provides nifty features such as zoom-in and zoom-out

- Google Maps is the 500-pound gorilla and provides lots of added features such as data overlays

- For the law, envision a Legal Maps online system that was akin to the Google Maps aspects

- Boost the Legal Maps by also adding AI capabilities into the mix

Chapter 19 - AI & Law: Posthumanization

Key briefing points about this chapter:

- Legal personhood applies to a natural person or commonly expressed as a human being

- There is juridical personhood reserved for artificial persons

- Generally, there is a somewhat strident dichotomy of being able to differentiate those two

- A posthumanization era will portend a blurring of human versus non-human facets

- The act of "thinking" is an unlikely tiebreaker since AI will undercut that difference

Chapter 20 - AI & Law: AI Law Not Computable

Key briefing points about this chapter:

- There is abundant effort afoot to create and advance AI-based legal reasoning systems

- One vexing question is whether the law is ultimately a computable number or not

- This is a perhaps similar question posed about the field of mathematics

- Historically, the Church-Turing thesis or assertion is that mathematics is not computable per se

- Some legal scholars use the same logic and contend that law is limited in the same manner

Chapter 21 - AI & Law: Collective Intelligence

Key briefing points about this chapter:

- There is a field of study known as "collective intelligence"

- When intelligence is collectively utilized, there is a chance of the sum being more than the parts

- AI is gradually embodying human intelligence and can aid the collective intelligence pursuits

- Envision too that AI will be operating in the legal field

- This gives rise to exploring a future of AI-based collective intelligence in the law

Chapter 22 – AI & Law: Limits Of Human Mind

Key briefing points about this chapter:

- The human brain weighs about 3 pounds and presumably is duly constrained in its size

- Some argue that our "minds" have used the entirety of the brain and we are at our limits

- Such an argument was made about the field of mathematics and might apply to the law too

- But efforts to formulate AI-based legal reasoning might take us to the next level

- And AI might advance legal reasoning, even if the human mind remains constrained

Chapter 23 - AI & Law: Judicial Machine Readability

Key briefing points about this chapter:

- Judicial opinions can be tough to figure out and the writing style is often obtuse

- There have been ongoing calls for judges and courts to write in a more human-readable way

- More recently, there are calls for judicial decisions to be made readily machine-readable

- Part of the basis for wanting machine readability would be to aid AI-based legal reasoning

- Whether judicial decisions will change in style and wording seems like an uphill battle

Chapter 24 - AI & Law: Legal Ecosystem

Key briefing points about this chapter:

- Ecosystems are complex and involve complicated intricacies

- Yellowstone National Park provides an exemplar of biological ecosystem complexities

- Analogously, the law and practice of law can be viewed as the legal ecosystem

- When a change is made to one part of the legal ecosystem this can induce cascading impacts

- It will be important for AI to be considered as a novel change across the entire legal ecosystem

Chapter 25 - AI & Law: Oxford – Levels Of Autonomy

Key briefing points about this article:

- Not all AI systems are the same in the sense of achieving autonomy (some less so, some more so)

- There are various level of autonomy that have been devised for autonomous vehicles

- Those levels can be adjusted and applied to AI legal reasoning

- A proposed set of levels of autonomy for AI legal reasoning are proffered herein

- The levels would be quite useful for legal scholars, academics and for attorneys and other practitioners in the field of law

More About This Book

For anyone opting to use this book in a class or course that pertains to these topics, note that Appendix A contains suggestions about how to use the book in a classroom setting.

Furthermore, Appendix B contains a set of slides that depict many of the salient points made throughout the book.

In some of my prior books, I've interspersed the slides into the chapter contents, but feedback by readers has generally been that readers prefer to not have the textual flow become disrupted by the slides, and instead prefer to have the supplemental material assembled altogether into an appendix.

To make sure that you are aware of those added materials, you'll notice that the ending of each chapter provides a quick reminder about the visual depictions that are available in Appendix B.

And so, with this overall orientation to the nature and structure of this book in mind, please proceed to read the essays and learn about the field of AI and law. I'm truly hoping that you'll find the essays mentally engaging and stimulative to the nature of how the law is being practiced and what the future of the law might become.

Note: *For supplemental materials depicting the aspects discussed in this chapter, refer to Appendix B, which contains various augmented diagrams, charts, and additional related facets of relevance.*

CHAPTER 2

AI & LAW: ECHO CHAMBERS IN THE LAW

Key briefing points about this essay:

- It is common to refer to those that hear and see the same thing to be in an echo chamber

- There is a squelching of other ideas that takes place, purposely or by happenstance

- At times there are attorneys in say a law firm that can get themselves into an echo chamber

- Echo chambers have some benefits but also can be at the cost of new ideas

- The advent of AI-based legal reasoning could be an interloper to disrupt such echoes

Introduction

It used to be that whenever someone mentioned an echo chamber, you knew they were referring to musical producers or musicians that used a specialized chamber to help devise their audio recordings. Nowadays, the echo chamber has taken on a new life and a somewhat different kind of meaning (though retaining the functional essence, one might contend).

We are abundantly growing accustomed to conceptually repurposing the vaunted "echo chamber" to highlight circumstances whereby those in a particular bubble are likely to hear and read the same comments and points of view that they already espoused. This is a variant of groupthink, another popularized term though one that seems to have lost traction in modern times, involving those that think alike becoming enamored of only others that think the same way they do (or, at least going along without speaking out of tune).

You might be somewhat offended that just because you prefer a particular topic or perspective that it gets summarily denigrated by tagging it with the sourness of being an instance of yet another echo chamber. If you are someone that loves wine, and you relish speaking, meeting, and sharing glasses of wine with others, you can be accused of being in a wine-oriented echo chamber.

One supposes this could be problematic if say the only wine you'll discuss is red wine, and no one in this wine connoisseur's encampment is willing or daring enough to proffer the benefits of white wines. It could be that the absence of even mentioning anything other than red wine will deny you the awareness of something equally valuable and beneficial. Your efforts to keep all other perspectives at bay, whether by design or by happenstance, can be your own loss and potential defeat.

This can happen to lawyers too.

Not about the wine, but about the notion of forming an echo chamber amongst those partners in your law firm and having a default barrier to avert hearing or considering other legal viewpoints beyond those of your bubble at hand. You might deliberately craft such a bubble, doing so with a specific grand purpose and the expectation that birds of a feather ought to naturally flock together.

Or the bubble might organically seem to take shape. No one was going out of their way to get into the same echo chamber, it just managed to occur by a process of viewpoint osmosis.

Okay, so let's agree that echo chambers can be advantageous to the degree that they can enable those of common interest to have a devoted machination that supports their focus. This can make life easier to stay within a particular groove and stay attuned to that topic. Let's also then willingly agree that a downside is a chance of becoming myopic and failing to know or detect when the echoing has drowned out new ideas or better ways of getting things done.

How can an echo chambered collection of acutely aligned attorneys break out of the resounding echoes to ascertain whether they are missing the boat or potentially are all aiming to stride over the edge of the same legal cliff?

Someone, or something, has to be willing to try and pierce into the echo chamber, though it won't be easy and there is a hefty probability of a swift backlash toward any such intrusions.

Maybe instead of a human taking such an ostracizing chance at this interloping act, we could use AI to do so.

Say what?

Let's take a moment to quickly get up-to-speed about AI and the law, and then we can return to those feisty breakouts.

AI as the Echo Chamber Buster

There is an ever-increasing pursuit of applying AI to the practice of law. This includes using the latest in Natural Language Processing to try and analyze legal documents and ferret out embedded legal arguments and possible loopholes. Another AI approach involves using Machine Learning, a computational pattern matching facility that can try and find appropriate precedents in a vast corpus of existing legal cases. And so on.

Gradually, the hope is to advance the AI toward being semi-autonomous when it comes to doing legal reasoning.

An attorney would have at their beck and call a handy online AI legal reasoning system that could enable them to bounce legal ideas off of, trying to figure out the best legal strategies for tackling a thorny case. It is anticipated that eventually this kind of AI will be expanded to become autonomous in capabilities and could possibly render legal advice without the need for being paired with a human lawyer.

With that preamble, now consider the revered but possibly flawed instances of a legally minded echo chamber amongst a collective set of human attorneys.

Those attorneys might eventually be leveraging an AI legal reasoning system, which could detect too that they are all thinking alike and only fueling among themselves the same kind of legal arguments and legal postures. The AI could spark their realization of this echo chamber immersion and spur them to explore other legal angles they otherwise would not have heard in their deafening echoes.

If a human attorney tried to get the echo chamber collective to wake-up and smell the roses, there is a darned good chance that the attorney would be tossed out of the collective and be cast aside as a rebel and, well, an outright outcast. On the other hand, the odds are that if the AI does the same intrusion, few would decide it is time to pull the plug on the AI (though the AI will certainly need to be watchful of such an outcome, I say with a bit of tongue in cheek).

Thus, one notable benefit for human lawyers using robust AI-based legal reasoning would be to proffer new ways of thinking about legal tactics and strategies and help to overcome a semblance of either groupthink or crack open a proverbial echo chamber that might be clouding and preventing innovative viewpoints.

Conclusion

It might be nice to leave the matter at that satisfying result, though there is one added twist. In theory, the AI itself might get into its own variant of an echo chamber, and possibly reinforce the one that the human attorneys have already formulated.

Perhaps a crafty human attorney would politely let the AI know and help it become a freer thinker.

––––––––––––

Note: *For supplemental materials depicting the aspects discussed in this chapter, refer to Appendix B, which contains various augmented diagrams, charts, and additional related facets of relevance*

CHAPTER 3
AI & LAW:
ROLE REVERSIBLE
JUDGMENT

Key briefing points about this essay:

- AI is increasingly being infused into the practice of law

- A great deal of debate centers on whether AI will be suitable in the role of judges

- One argument is that AI won't have a first-person perspective and only third-person

- Without the capacity to walk in the shoes of another there is concern over AI judgments

- Counterarguments include AI as judicial neutrality, plus AI embodiment of sentimentality

Introduction

Are you able to see the world through the eyes of others?

Some believe that only those with an empathetic bent can best serve in the role of an attorney or that of a judge. Humans can comprehend what other humans are feeling and what they are enduring. Presumably, this is hidden and an assumed requisite for serving in the law and only found in humans, ostensibly lacking in automation.

This brings up a brewing battle about the possibility of AI becoming integral to the practice of law. Generally, AI and the law are envisioned as two peas in a pod, providing significant benefits for each other. Unfortunately, there might be a fly in the ointment such that the AI part of the equation hits a proverbial wall and can go no further in terms of providing a completely capable and independent facility for performing legal tasks.

As background, before we take a look at the detrimental bee in the bonnet, let's cover a few essentials about AI and the law. Experts predict that the use of AI in the practice of law will eventually become vital for lawyers as they prepare for and argue their cases, and so too will AI be key in adjudication as judges leverage AI-based legal reasoning systems for the crafting of court rulings.

Initially, AI infusion will be relatively modest and merely provide a handy add-on to the judicial process, although not proffering a particularly demonstrative difference. Advances in AI will increasingly enable a wider array of capabilities and thus AI-based legal reasoning will improve substantially. This in turn will lead to a greater reliance on semi-autonomous legal reasoning systems that work somewhat hand-in-hand with human legal professionals. Ultimately, there is the possibility for fully autonomous AI legal reasoning systems to emerge, ones that can practice law ably and do so without the need for human legal handholding.

Along that rather arduous path toward a totality of meshing the law and AI, there is one gotcha that some contend will be a stumbling block that cannot be overcome. In brief, it has to do with the difference between being in the third-person versus being in the first-person. The crux of the argument about AI reaching a pinnacle of the law is that it will always be stuck at the third-person perspective of existence and never progress into the first-person viewpoint.

Seems somewhat mystical, I realize.

Let's take a moment to unpack the contention to figure out what this all entails.

AI And The Shoes Of Mankind

A scholarly research paper that appeared in the *Oklahoma Law Review* provides a helpful basis for exploring this third-person versus first-person conundrum (the piece was published in 2019, Volume 27, Number 1). Authored by Professor Joshua Davis, serving in the School of Law at the University of San Francisco and also Director at their Center for Law and Ethics, he postulated in his piece entitled "Artificial Wisdom? A Potential Limit On AI In Law (And Elsewhere)" that AI is going to eventually have an especially rough time succeeding in the legal field.

He emphasized that the rutty road emanates from the asserted contention that AI is exclusively scientific-minded, as it were, and will ergo only imbue a third-person viewpoint of the world: "Two characteristics—likely related—mark AI. First, it appears to operate purely in the realm of the scientific world. The knowledge it captures is most consistent with a naturalized materialism—with a popular understanding of science. Second, at least as far as we know, AI inhabits a third-person perspective."

Let's assume this conjectured emphasis is apt, for the moment (we'll revisit this in my closing remarks).

Where this raises troubles for AI in the law is that a third-person perspective is ostensibly outside of the law as though a kind of overseer or observer and lacks a direct and introspective capacity to understand what it is like to be subject to the law.

In essence, all of us, including lawyers, judges, and all legal professionals are not only able to see the law in a third-person manner, but also experience the law in a veritable first-person fashion too, as stated in the research: "It may be that AI is limited to the realm of science, that science cannot fully capture the first-person perspective, that the first-person perspective is necessary to make moral judgments, and that legal and judicial practitioners sometimes must make moral judgments. If all of that proves true, we may have identified a bulwark against AI taking over all aspects of our legal system."

You might refer to this as not being able to walk in the shoes of another.

A famous phrasing brings this to clarity, per the paper: "In that sense, the law is 'self-imposed.' A judge—or, again, potentially a lawyer—must be able to say, 'There but for the grace of God go I' (or the secular equivalent). They characterize their position as requiring 'role-reversible judgment.' "

Let's narrow our focus solely on judges and consider the notion of this role-reversible capacity.

A judge might contemplate what they would want as an outcome to a court case if they were in the shoes of the parties involved. The judge could mull over the possibility that were it not for the hand of fate, they might be sitting there in court and be the one facing the bench. So, if AI-based legal reasoning systems are going to be eventually in the role of a judge in our courts, can the AI truly put itself into those shoes and ask itself the same introspective and altogether meditative questions?

Assuming that the envisioned future AI cannot do so, this suggests that we not ought to let AI sit upon the bench, at least absent of a human judge seated there too to provide the needed first-person ingredient.

Not everyone concurs with this potential AI legal systems spoiler.

For example, one argument is that we don't want judges to be sitting in the shoes of someone else. Are they wearing the shoes of the defendant, and only seeing the case through those eyes? What about the other party in the case? Is it possible to wear all those shoes and reconcile them (seems unlikely)? Some assert that a judge should try to remain impartial and dispassionate, for which wearing any shoes other than those of the judge would be tantamount to undue tainting.

In a semblance of seeking abject judicial neutrality, you could even argue that the AI will be a better choice as an adjudicating decision-maker since human judges are susceptible to putting themselves into the shoes of their fellow humans.

Of course, the core assumption throughout this presumed dilemma is that AI cannot achieve the first-person capacity. Notably, there are ongoing attempts at embodying a kind of simulated empathy into AI systems. Whether this simulated feature is identical to the human variant can be heartedly questioned, though the point being that we might be able to ensure that the AI is first-person capable.

Conclusion

As a result of this simulated facet, the third-person versus first-person debate would dissolve and no longer be the impenetrable barrier for AI-based legal reasoning. You could counterargue that the AI might be a type of blessing in disguise, being able to overcome the "but for the hand of fate, go I" potential ethical morass.

Well, at least until the day that AI gains sentience and in that case, one supposes we can only hope that the AI will try to see the world in the shoes of humanity.

Note: *For supplemental materials depicting the aspects discussed in this chapter, refer to Appendix B, which contains various augmented diagrams, charts, and additional related facets of relevance.*

CHAPTER 4

AI & LAW:

WHEN AI IS THE CRIMINAL

Key briefing points about this essay:

- There is eagerness in using AI for the betterment of humanity

- Though not as apparent is the use of AI for committing criminal acts

- If a human crook employs AI for illegal efforts there is still a human responsible

- Not so clearcut is what to do when the AI morphs from good to bad and commits crimes

- Some wonder whether existing laws will be able to contend with AI as the crook

Introduction

Fortunately, so far, most of what AI systems are doing is usually for a relatively good or favorable reason. AI is being applied to speed-up manufacturing. AI is used to aid in financial matters. The United Nations has emphasized that AI can be used for the betterment of humanity in many crucial ways. These are all considered part of the *AI For Good* camp.

That's all certainly a healthy and heartwarming aspiration.

Not as frequently heard about or even particularly discussed is the *AI For Bad*.

Yes, whenever there is something that can be applied to the goodness of mankind there is usually ample room to apply that same innovation to the ugly underbelly of society. AI can be used by bad people to do bad things. This is not something that many touting AI want to necessarily bring up. It is decidedly bad public relations for AI.

I'm sure that once AI starts to get abundantly used by crooks and for illegal dealings, the word about how AI has been shunted over into the *AI For Bad* camp is going to being to spread. People will clamor for ways to prevent or mitigate the untoward use of AI. Technological means of controlling the AI are certainly going to be sought and utilized.

Of course, the law proffers another means to cope with AI that is being used for foul play.

We need to consider the use case of when AI is a criminal.

Might as well start lining up to deal with the problem while it is still in a nascent state.

One of the forerunner research papers on this topic was published in 2018, seemingly eons ago in the rapid pace of AI these days. Authored by faculty at Oxford University and from elsewhere, the provocative piece was entitled "Artificial Intelligence Crime: An Interdisciplinary Analysis of Foreseeable Threats and Solutions" (written by Thomas C. King, Nikita Aggarwal, Mariarosaria Taddeo, and Luciano Floridi, as published in *Science and Engineering Ethics*).

There are some important facets to establish when discussing the AI-Crime (AIC) topic.

First, you could easily point to misuses of AI that go back to the start of the AI field, ostensibly beginning in the 1950s or so.

This showcases that there isn't something especially new about exploiting AI techniques and technologies for the performance of criminal acts. That's pretty much a given.

Second, the recent recasting of the *AI as a crook* mantra is that we need to differentiate between the use of AI as a mere happenstance or optional means of committing the crime versus the AI being a core and essential element of the illegal effort. In other words, the focus is on crime that depended upon the AI and for which without the AI the unlawful acts were unlikely to have been carried out.

Third, the AI being used is considered bona fide AI and not just some ramshackle automation that one might try to tag the AI moniker onto. Here, this is the idea that the AI did things that only AI can do, and that presumably non-AI technology could not do. Do not over-interpret that point. The AI can be using conventional technologies, so the use of ordinary stuff does not discount the AI tagging, but there must be something about the criminal effort that genuinely uses AI and not solely everyday tech.

In case you are wondering about the preceding points as being ironclad, the answer to that unspoken question is that there is lots of wiggle room in there. Enough flexible space that it is not going to be an easy one to pin down in a legal sense of seeking definitiveness.

The rule-of-thumb or north-star here is that the crime could not have occurred were it not for the hand of AI, so to speak.

Can AI Be Held Responsible

Why is this such a seemingly important distinction?

This takes us to the rub.

It is conceivable that we will potentially end-up with circumstances whereby the AI is the criminal. What this signifies is that there might not be a human attributable to the crime, and all we have is the AI that committed the crime, on its own, and nary a human crook involved (i.e., not a hidden human, none at all).

The foreboding question arises like this: *Can we assert that the AI itself is subject to a criminal act, and if so, will our existing laws allow for an AI system to be prosecuted for said crimes?*

The initial reaction from most real-world hardened lawyers is that this is pure nonsense to suggest that the AI did something, on its own and therefore can or should be held responsible as though it possesses some form of legal personhood. Presumably, at some prior point in time, a human started the snowball of somehow crafting or launching the AI. You can't let that crook or criminal mastermind hide from the responsibility and simply point to some disembodied AI as the culprit to be nabbed.

Well, these are all heated and fighting words, to be sure.

According to the research paper: 'Liability refers to the concern that AIC could undermine existing liability models, thereby threatening the dissuasive and redressing power of the law. Existing liability models may be inadequate to address the future role of AI in criminal activities. The limits of the liability models may therefore undermine the certainty of the law, as it may be the case that agents, artificial or otherwise, may perform criminal acts or omissions without sufficient concurrence with the conditions of liability for a particular offence to constitute a (specifically) criminal offence."

Some assuredly acknowledge that there is undoubtedly AI that is devised by evildoers to do evil acts. Those evildoers should be traced to the AI actions and be held responsible for what they have unleashed. That case is closed, one might say.

But what about AI that transformed upon itself and (let's assume) inadvertently went down the path of crime? Suppose that an altogether *AI For Good* system that was helping to cope with the pandemic had morphed into a privacy intruding criminal system that also stole people's identities, perhaps creating DeepFakes that looked like those innocents and used the result to commit crimes of theft, fraud, or the like.

The counterargument to these nefarious scenarios is that this presumes a sentient AI. To be clear and ostensibly inarguable as a point of reference, there is no AI that today exhibits anything at all like sentience, and we do not know if this will be feasible, either in the long-term or even ever.

Conclusion

These are open-ended concerns and time will tell how this shakes out.

Meanwhile, some are wringing their hands that this might mean that human criminals will be deskilled, having allowed their criminal wherewithal to dissipate as they become lax and let the AI do the heavyweight crookery for them (all part of the criminal sharing economy).

Now that's a twist.

Note: *For supplemental materials depicting the aspects discussed in this chapter, refer to Appendix B, which contains various augmented diagrams, charts, and additional related facets of relevance.*

CHAPTER 5
AI & LAW:
APOLOGETIC AI
LEGAL TROUBLES

Key briefing points about this essay:

- AI systems are increasingly being programmed to emit apologies

- Some like the apology and feel better, while others find it insulting and a hollow gesture

- There is a substantial body of legal literature on the topic of law-and-apologies

- In some respects, an apology is legally exculpatory and in other ways legally inculpatory

- Firms making AI might be digging themselves a hole, plus AI liability could later arise

Introduction

Are you the type of person that expects to get an apology when someone else has done something wrong or that you feel otherwise owes you an act of contrition?

If so, you'll be glad to know that AI systems are increasingly emitting a sorrowful response when they have done something that you don't like or that has potentially hurt your feelings. That being said, keep in mind that today's AI is not sentient and nor even close to reaching such a vaunted pinnacle. The apologetic AI being fostered onto the world currently is AI that has been programmed to emit an apology wherein the software developers have predetermined that an apology seems warranted.

For example, you apply for a car loan from an AI-based online system and the underlying Machine Learning algorithms determine that you are unworthy of being granted a loan. Rather than merely informing you that you have been rejected, the AI then also produces a kind-of apology that says the decision is quite regretful and hopefully you are not overly dismayed at the result. In essence, the AI is sorry to have cast you asunder.

Would such an apology soothe your bruised self-esteem and perhaps materially soften the abject disappointment at not getting the loan?

Maybe, at least that's what the AI developers assume will happen.

On the other hand, some believe that the apology is akin to adding salt into the wounds of your denunciation. It is one thing to have a human provide a heartfelt apology, and altogether insulting to have a machine appear to be sorrowful. This seems like a hollow gesture and aims at those that do not realize that today's AI is dense as a brick and utterly unlike human mental acumen.

Some decry this AI is fooling the public by seeming to have intelligence that it just doesn't possess.

As people get used to seeing these apologies, they will further anthropomorphize the AI and fall down a slippery slope of being deceived into believing that the AI is pretty much a humanoid.

The Legal Apologies Conundrum

From a legal perspective, there is another insightful point to be made.

The old maxim is that liability means never being able to say that you are sorry.

For those of you not especially familiar with the law-and-apology field of study, there is a storied history of how apologies, encompassing those made by humans and ostensibly by non-living entities such as corporations, have been treated by the law. One of my favorite recent articles covering this topic was authored by John Kleefeld and entitled "Promoting and Protecting Apologetic Discourse through Law: A Global Survey and Critique of Apology Legislation and Case Law" (appeared in Volume 7, Number 3, 2017 issue of *Onati Socio-Legal Series*).

In the United States, a landmark state law covering apologies was enacted in 1986 when a Massachusetts senator led and got passed a bill that was prompted by the fact that his daughter was killed by a car driver and the driver had said he wanted to apologize but was fearful of the legal consequences by doing so.

Researcher Kleefeld describes the apologies conundrum this way: "This view arises from the general rule that a party's out-of-court statement or conduct against interest, not otherwise protected by privilege (e.g., the privilege associated with settlement discussions), is admissible against that party at trial even though it would otherwise be excluded as hearsay evidence. The Massachusetts bill sought to provide a 'safe harbor' for such would-be apologizers by rendering their sympathetic words or 'benevolent gestures' inadmissible in a civil action, and spawned comparative initiatives in almost every US state."

Of course, lawyers and judges have been arguing about the nature of what constitutes an apology, doing so since perhaps the invention of adjudication. There are disputes over the scope and boundaries of an apologetic statement or utterance.

This can be significant since it then shapes whether the apology gets into court or does not get included.

Generally, the rule-of-thumb is that an apology is composed of remorse, responsibility, resolution, and reparation, the so-called four Rs of legally defined apologetic expressions. If you merely tell someone you are sorry, this presumably is insufficient as a legally recognizable apology since it lacks or renders ambiguous at least three of the Rs.

Some assert that legislating the nature of apologies is good because it enables those that wish to apologize for the legal latitude to do so, and might therefore lead to the resolving of civil disputes in a more efficacious way. As per Kleefeld: "British Columbia's *Apology Act*, or its model-act equivalent in Canada, the *Uniform Apology Act*, aims to do this for civil disputes generally. Other statutory provisions, notably in the US, aim to do this in the health care context."

A reader of my column, lawyer Joseph McMenamin and a professor in the Department of Legal Medicine at Virginia Commonwealth University, brought to my attention the Virginia law encompassing health care providers and apologies, providing a handy example of such legal language, as stated in Virginia's *Death By Wrongful Act* "the portion of statements, writings, affirmations, benevolent conduct, or benevolent gestures expressing sympathy, commiseration, condolence, compassion, or a general sense of benevolence, together with apologies that are made by a health care provider or an agent of a health care provider to a relative of the patient, or a representative of the patient about the death of the patient as a result of the unanticipated outcome of health care, shall be inadmissible as evidence of an admission of liability or as evidence of an admission against interest."

Well, one thing to realize is that not everyone sees apologies as being quite so beneficial.

Some argue an apology is bound to set ablaze a matter that might otherwise not have risen to the level of being played out in the courts.

The person receiving the apology is apt to feel that they got a clear cut acknowledgment of wrongdoing that was done to them, and therefore be spurred to file a legal case accordingly.

Another twist is that some laws make exculpatory the part of the apology that seems heartfelt, and establishes that inculpatory is the part that appears to be an admission of guilt. This then leaves juries with the impression that the apologizer seemingly admitted they were at fault and furthermore refused to express sorrowfulness for doing so.

Conclusion

In any case, we are likely to soon see that the AI-powered apologies open up another can of worms in the law-and-apology field. If there is any shift toward AI gaining a smidgeon of legal personhood, where then does the apology issued by an AI semi-autonomous or fully autonomous system land?

Being watchful of apologizing might be a savvy move, and the cutting remarks by Oliver Wendell Holmes, Sr. come to mind as added basis to avert proffering an apology: "Apology is only egotism wrong side out.".

Note: *For supplemental materials depicting the aspects discussed in this chapter, refer to Appendix B, which contains various augmented diagrams, charts, and additional related facets of relevance.*

CHAPTER 6
AI & LAW:
PERSONAL DIGITAL IDENTITY

Key briefing points about this essay:

- A recent class session of the MIT Computational Law 2021 course discussed digital identity

- Included were Wyoming State Senator Chris Rothfuss and personal digital identity legislation

- The approach reflects the legal notion of personal digital identity as a bundled agency

- In addition to sorely needed legal imbuements, the role of AI-based enablement can add value

- Envision a layer of self-governing digital identity being run by an AI system on your behalf

Introduction

One of the most exasperating and distressing aspects of modern-day life is the use and misuse of your personal digital identity.

We are regrettably accustomed to being worried night-and-day about how our personal data such as date of birth and social security number are at risk of exploitation for identity theft purposes.

45

Whenever a website asks for personal info, you likely cringe and have to soberly reflect whether the danger of sharing the data is worth whatever benefit you'll derive from providing it.

Numerous legal frameworks have been popping out of the woodwork in hopes of getting a handle on the societal angst over the use and personal control of our digital identifiers. Sometimes referred to as digital assets governance, the notion is to legally establish some systematic and explicit approaches to that which otherwise has been somewhat left to the winds and whims of a laissez-faire digital world.

It is no easy legal feat to get one's arms fully around the digital identity realm as there are numerous potential gotchas and semantically indeterminate loopholes that make for a quite slippery conundrum.

Nonetheless, valiant efforts to find the right legislative and legally robust brew are underway.

A recent class session of the MIT Computational Law 2021 course included Wyoming State Senator Chris Rothfuss to discuss the groundbreaking legislative efforts on digital identity that are underway in Wyoming (recall, the official state nickname is in fact the Equality State). The session was superbly moderated by Dazza Greenwood, research scientist and lecturer at the MIT Media Lab, along with co-host Bryan Wilson, MIT Fellow, and showcased the hard work of Senator Rothfuss and the Select Committee on Blockchain, Financial Technology, and Digital Innovation Technology (available online as Senate File No. SF0039).

Here is the cornerstone definition of personal digital identity contained in the Act: " 'Personal digital identity' means the intangible digital representation of, by and for a natural person, over which he has dominion and through which he intentionally communicates or acts" (the legislation intends that the gender pronoun is he/she/they).

Furthermore, this is the sovereign connecting bridge of the personal digital identity and the represented natural person: "Acts taken through a personal digital identity are attributable to a natural person if they were the act of the natural person. The act of the natural person may be established in any manner, including a showing of the efficacy of any security procedure applied to determine the natural person to which an electronic record or electronic signature or other act was attributable."

In a nutshell, a crucial conceptual interpretation is to envision that your personal digital identity is somewhat of its own capacity and presumably acts on your personal behalf. You and your personal digital identity are still one and unified, yet there is a thing or entity that exists as your digital representation and that is not merely static but also dynamic in its nature.

For those of you that are versed in this area of the law, you might recall the work by researcher Dr. Clare Sullivan at the University of Adelaide in the excellent treatise entitled *Digital Identity* published in 2011. A crucial question is addressed as to whether it might be sensible and useful to consider that your digital identity has some semblance of legal personhood: "It is a departure from the familiar to assert that there is an emergent legal concept of identity which is comprised purely of a set of information, let alone to assert that it is endowed with legal personality."

Per Sullivan's research, this possibility does not seem quite as farfetched as it might seem at first glance:
"However, when viewed from the perspective of other disciplines such as computer science, the notion that information has function as well as meaning is well established, as is machine intelligence whereby computers can make decisions and, indeed, act much like a human being." This is similar to the notions explored by Daniel Solove in his 2004 book "The Digital Person, Technology and Privacy in the Information Age."

Note carefully that the aspect of machine intelligence subtly arose in the preceding quoted remark.

As readers of my writings are well aware, I've covered various elements underlying the AI-as-legal-personhood debate.

You can add to this growing haystack the idea of layering natural legal personhood with the *surround sound* of a self-governing personal digital identity, for which AI could make such a machination more readily attainable.

AI Enablement Of Personal Digital Identity

Envision that there is an AI-based autonomous system that encapsulates your human-focused personal digital identity.

The AI is effectively your agent, your power of attorney, if you will, acting on your behalf to ascertain and attempt to monitor and control where your digital identity goes and how it is used. Working on a relentless 24x7 basis, the AI is continually seeking to find ways to ensure that your personal digital identity is not misused, and furthermore (if desired by you) attempts to discover ways to leverage your digital identity to your personal advantage.

The logic for why AI comes to the forefront is that otherwise there is a somewhat toothless mechanism for both protecting and fostering your personal digital identity. Contemporary personal digital identity consists of shards of digital loose ends that are without any facility to act on their own. They lay around, vulnerable to all those that happen upon the bits and bytes, and opt to exploit the unprotected treasure. Though having laws to govern such use are indeed vital, on a practical basis there needs to be a means of implementing a dynamic and responsive milieu of your digital identity and not leave it simply feebly motionless and highly vulnerable.

To clarify, this use of AI does not rely upon somehow reaching the vaunted pinnacle of AI-based sentience. We are not at sentience as yet and it is an open question as to when, or if ever, such a day will arrive. Thus, if sentience was a necessity in this cause, you might as well drop the notion altogether.

Conclusion

AI in a semi-autonomous capacity could suffice as the guardian for your personal digital identity. Armed with the legal wherewithal about how your digital identity is to be protected and also can be proffered, the AI would steadfastly represent your digital representation.

This provides a one-two punch, namely laws to provide the needed underpinning, and the AI acting to uphold those laws and being your online sheriff doing its duty around the clock and around the electronic globe.

Note: *For supplemental materials depicting the aspects discussed in this chapter, refer to Appendix B, which contains various augmented diagrams, charts, and additional related facets of relevance.*

CHAPTER 7

AI & LAW:

STOCKPILING LEGAL POSTURES

Key briefing points about this essay:

- Lawyers create legal arguments and must do so with moves and countermoves in mind

- AI-based legal reasoning systems will gradually augment those laborious efforts

- Imagine the AI as a kind-of chess-playing capability though in the realm of legal arguments

- You could potentially have the AI generate a slew of newly minted legal arguments

- If so, should they be made open to all or can you keep them a secret (an ethical dilemma)

Introduction

There is the famous children's allegory about the little red hen that goes to the trouble to bake bread, doing so all alone, and then must decide whether to share the bread with others that wish to have some of it.

One perspective is that this story illustrates that to the victor, should go the spoils (or, perhaps, alternatively, for those that put in the time and energy, they should bear the fruits of their labors).

However you view the matter, it certainly raises thorny ethical questions.

Consider an emerging ethical dilemma that some foresee arising in an era of AI-powered legal reasoning.

First, some key background.

Artificial Intelligence (AI) is gradually and inexorably entering into the legal profession.

There is the use of Natural Language Processing (NLP), which we already experience in everyday ordinary interaction with Alexa and Siri and has been increasingly added into various LegalTech systems such as used for contract management, e-Discovery, and the like. Another avenue of AI consists of Machine Learning and Deep Learning. These computational pattern matching techniques are being used to predict court rulings and are also employed to ferret out prior relevant cases amongst a large-scale corpus of online court records.

One of the most fascinating and likely law-disruptive AI technologies involves AI-based legal reasoning systems.

The notion is that the AI simulates the legal argumentation precepts of human attorneys and essentially carries out a limited form of legal reasoning.

Initially, these AI-based legal reasoners would be used as an aid for lawyers and jurists seeking to craft legal arguments. In this semi-autonomous mode, the AI works hand-in-hand with the human legal expert and they jointly establish a robust legal argument or legal posture. Some assert that this capability by the AI will inevitably be further advanced and we will have available fully autonomous AI-based legal reasoning systems that can act in lieu of needing any human legal guidance.

Stockpiling Chess Moves And Legal Arguments

An easy way to envision this legal argumentation creation is to imagine a game of chess that involves making legal moves rather than conventional chessboard moves.

Chess players are apt to try and think ahead as to what move their adversary will make. Legal arguments are somewhat the same in that it is important for a lawyer to consider their legal stance and how the opposing counsel will attempt to counter every legal assertion being made. The legal posture that an attorney ultimately composes ought to have numerous legal points that are readied for counterarguments. Furthermore, those expected counterarguments should have been already assessed, thus having in-hand readymade counters to those counterarguments. And so on, nesting as deeply as needed for the case at hand.

Assume that an AI-based legal reasoning system is at your fingertips and able to churn through the mounds upon mounds of potential legal arguments for a new case that you are working on.

This computational legal beagle can identify all potential legal arguments. Out of this wide search space of legal wrangling, the AI narrows the possibilities by identifying spurious arguments that are unworthy of consideration. The remaining tightened set is further refined. All possible counterarguments are electronically evaluated to ascertain which are likely to hold water and which would potentially sink the ship if used against you. Voila, after an extended period of time to calculate all of this, out pops the most favorable and strongest argument to be put forth for your case.

You would undoubtedly proceed to use the legal posture and be relatively confident that your adversary will find themselves on the losing end of the legal stick, as it were.

In this example, you were faced with an existing legal case and decided to have the AI-based legal reasoning system punch through a vast legal search space of possible moves and countermoves.

That is a one-time use of such a system. But there's no reason that you might only use the system in that ostensibly singular way.

Suppose you let loose the computational facility and have it explore a wide variety of legal cases that pertain to whatever legal specialty you focus on, including theoretical cases that no one has yet ever seen. The system processing time might take many hours, days, weeks, or perhaps even months for the AI to sufficiently and exhaustingly examine and assess. It would be like having a chess-playing system that tries to discover and assess a huge number of possible playing chess board positions, strategies, and tactics, requiring a tremendous amount of calculative muscle and processing time to undertake.

Okay, after letting the AI legal reasoning system crank along, you now have in-hand all of these pre-mapped legal arguments and legal postures.

What shall you do with them?

One possible answer is to stockpile them.

Keep them in your back pocket. Save them for a rainy day. For those legal arguments in the devised set that have not yet seen the light of day, they are your readymade "gotcha's" that can be used whenever such a case appears. You now hold the ace cards and can spring them forth when the right time arises.

Some argue that ethically you ought to divulge them.

Rather than sitting quietly upon a treasure trove of legal arguments, you should make them available for all. Society as a whole would be benefited.

The legal world would have a greater grasp of legal arguments that are potential to be made. Everyone seemingly comes out ahead.

Well, except that you presumably incurred the cost to have the AI-based legal reasoning system produce these to-date undisclosed legal postures. Seems like it should be your own Intellectual Property that for the time being is proprietary to your efforts and that of your law firm.

To which do you have a greater duty, the auspices of your own legal efforts or to the legal profession as a whole in terms of aiding the overall semblance of legal knowledge?

This somewhat dovetails into an ongoing debate in the computer field over open-source code versus programming code that is kept hidden and considered proprietary. If you wish to consider the law as a form or variant of code, there is a like question about whether the law and its codification in the realm of legal arguments is something that should always be open to all or whether it is satisfactory (and ethically pure) to keep it private.

Conclusion

Just as people use their computers to mine for cryptocurrency such as Bitcoin, perhaps we will experience lawyers and non-lawyers alike running AI-based legal reasoning systems to reveal new legal arguments. Those would either be altruistically shared or possibly become a highly prized treasure for the highest bidders that wish to bid on it.

Note: *For supplemental materials depicting the aspects discussed in this chapter, refer to Appendix B, which contains various augmented diagrams, charts, and additional related facets of relevance.*

CHAPTER 8

AI & LAW:

LAW AS CODE

Key briefing points about this essay:

- There is a great deal of effort aiming toward "law as code" (it is headline-making)

- The gist is to somehow convert laws into programming code, allowing for digital usage

- This is much more than simply textual aspects and requires runnable capacities too

- A tremendous stumbling block is the inherent semantic indeterminism of the law

- Suggestions that we change our laws to be amenable to coding are brazen and unlikely

Introduction

Law as code.

You are likely to see references to the popular phrase "law as code" in nearly any legal industry newspaper or social media posting that foretells the future of the law.

Generally, the notion underlying law as code is that we ought to embody the law into some form of computer program coding and thus we will more readily be able to utilize and leverage the law via digital capabilities.

This abundantly makes sense.

Today's laws are only digitally proficient to the degree that we are increasingly able to post textual narratives and snippets online, but they lack any semblance of action or functionality per se. Text is flat and unmoving. Programming code offers the possibility of being active and performance-based.

Let's pursue that thinking a bit further.

By transforming the law into something more robust and able to be used for legal reasoning, we could use computers to aid lawyers and jurists in ways that are currently relatively untenable. The hope is that the law as code would be runnable, doing so in the same manner that you can run an everyday ordinary program or app on your laptop or smartphone.

Adding icing on top of this cake, we could potentially interject Artificial Intelligence (AI) into the embodiment of law as code too. Without AI, the rudimentary variant of law as code would consist of the law in disparately coded fragments and be somewhat scattered and only usable at a lower level of legal reasoning. Infusing AI would help in turning the fragments into a cohesive whole, as though a human lawyer was able to bring a bigger picture to the code and orchestrate it into larger legal arguments and legal postures.

Because the word "law" in the phrasing of law as code seems potentially confusing, suggesting merely the static text of laws, some prefer to speak of *rules as code*, a shorthand for legal rules as code. This clears up some of the wonderment as to why we cannot just dump the text of laws into computer databases and be done with the seemingly banal chore. The reason this is so darned hard is that the law consists of rules, sometimes readily apparent and in other instances hidden or insidiously assumed.

Referring to the law as legal rules is an important indicator and handily reveals why law as code has not yet been solved.

It is principally due to legal rules being semantically indeterminate.

What's that?

We all know that a so-called natural language such as English allows for tremendous latitude in what you mean when making statements of nearly any kind. Recall the legal arguments over the word "is" that took place about testimony given by President Clinton, and you immediately realize that words and sentences are imprecise and fluid in their semantic meaning. A more formal way to emphasize this vagueness or leeway is to say that English is semantically indeterminate. There is nearly always more room to be had in any utterance and we can attach or find meaning to our heart's content.

In fact, it is the role and duty of a lawyer to seek out that semantic indeterminate semblances of a case and leverage it within the confines of their responsibilities as an officer of the court.

The overarching point is that law as code, when cast more adroitly as legal rules as code, means that we want to take something as source input that is semantically indeterminate and convert or transform it into an equal in all respects that can be expressed and utilized in a computer. This usually implies that we have to resolve the indeterminate aspects since the resulting transformed law has to now be runnable such that it purports to exactly represent what the law portends.

That is the gotcha in law as code.

Semantics As Three Hundred Pound Gorilla

Semantics is a tall order, a grand hill to be climbed, a daunting challenge to be conquered.

Supreme Court Justice Felix Frankfurter had eloquently stated: "All our work, our whole life, is a matter of semantics because words are the tools with which we work, the material out of which laws are made, out of which the Constitution was written. Everything depends on our understanding of them. So it's useless to say, `Oh well, that's just a matter of semantics'" (as quoted in *Miller v. United States*, Civ. A. No. 66-188, April 19, 1967).

When a lawyer looks at a snippet of the law, they bring to the inspection an entire vastness of semantic understanding. Somehow, the knowledge or intelligence underlying that semantic "conversion" is needed when attempting to transform the law into a computer program code. Not only is the conversion per se arduous, the target language that the resulting code consists of will make-or-break the viability of such a conversion.

Anthropological studies rooted in the research of Professor Franz Boas have indicated that Eskimo-Aleut languages have many more words for "snow" than does conventional English (there is controversy on this point, but nonetheless meritoriously is worth considering). Trying to convert any of those words for snow into English entails adding a lot of additional wording to seemingly grasp the same connotation as the original word. Even by those supplemental words, the original semantic intent is generally lost or at least likely misshapen.

The same can happen when trying to generate law as code.

Some suggest that we ought to change how we craft the law. In essence, to make the conversion easier, simply change the way we use our natural language and how we express laws in English. Furthermore, this would presumably eliminate any ambiguity about the laws and make adjudication straightforward and decidedly crisp.

Conclusion

In the struggle between whether to get lawyers and jurists to entirely and forever forward craft and recraft the law so that it is amenable to coding, versus finding some as yet unknown way to programmatically translate the law into code, you would be safer to bet on the side of devising a clever approach to a likely AI-based converter rather than getting humans and human behavior on such a large scale to change.

Both of those approaches are hard, and so it is a proverbial question of the lesser of two evils as to which will rue the day.

————

Note: *For supplemental materials depicting the aspects discussed in this chapter, refer to Appendix B, which contains various augmented diagrams, charts, and additional related facets of relevance.*

CHAPTER 9

AI & LAW:

LAWYERS AS CODERS

Key briefing points about this essay:

- There is tremendous interest (and rancor) about the proposition of lawyers-as-coders

- Some assert that the future of the law and especially via AI will radically impact attorneys

- As such the argument exists that lawyers would be prudent to learn about coding

- Counterarguments are that lawyers should stick with their knitting and let coders code

- A recent webinar by Northwestern University is used herein to explore these tradeoffs

Introduction

Lawyers and coding.

The odds are that you've seen headlines stating that lawyers-as-coders is the latest and hottest trend.

If you've had a chance to mull over the notion, you are likely to have landed into one of three dominant categories. There are those lawyers that completely buy into the lawyers-as-coders proclamation and believe in it, fervently so. Meanwhile, some lawyers think the lawyers-as-coders is utterly preposterous and not worthy of even an iota of thought. The third category consists of those lawyers that are uncertain.

The fence-sitters are unsure of how valid the contention is.

Questions haunt them in the sense that if they do proceed into transforming themselves into being a lawyer that is a coder, maybe they've made a career-limiting choice and didn't even know it.

On the other hand, the classic FOMO (fear of missing out) provides a powerful allure, namely that if other lawyers are jumping into coding and programming, perhaps those not doing so will miss the boat.

Nobody wants to be the last non-coding lawyer and be caught adrift of everyone else.

Ongoing chatter about lawyers as coders has especially ratcheted up due to the emergence of Artificial Intelligence (AI). AI is becoming more feasible overall and particularly more pronounced in the field of law than just a few years ago.

Headlines blare incessantly that human lawyers will be augmented by AI-based legal reasoning systems, meaning that lawyers will seemingly have no choice but to work hand-in-hand with AI systems.

Furthermore, some predict that AI will eventually be proficient on an autonomous basis and ergo able to proffer legal advice and act in the capacity of a human lawyer. All in all, this seems to broadcast the warning that coding is coming toward the practice of law, whether you want it to do so or not.

Discussing Intelligently Lawyers-As-Coders

The lawyers-as-coder topic came up at an excellent recent webinar entitled "Artificial Intelligence and the Future of Lawyering and Law Firms," which was superbly led and moderated by legal scholar Daniel W. Linna Jr., Senior Lecturer & Director of Law and Technology Initiatives, Northwestern Pritzker School of Law & McCormick School of Engineering. Speakers included Stephen Poor, Partner and chair emeritus, Seyfarth (law firm), Mari Sako, Professor of Management Studies, Saïd Business School, University of Oxford, and Hyejin Youn, Assistant Professor of Management & Organizations, Kellogg School of Management.

The notion of lawyers-as-coders is a matter that I've frequently been asked about and have forthrightly commented on, so I'll provide herein a recap gist of both the remarks made during the Northwestern University sponsored webinar and add my commentary too. Rather than listing the pro's and con's in separate lists, I like to weave together the advantages and disadvantages involving the topic and find that this provides a more engaging dialogue-like conveyance of the thorny debate.

Buckle your seatbelt and get ready for a roller coaster ride.

First, one of the most common and powerfully exhorted claims in opposition of lawyers-as-coders is this: A lawyer is paid to know about the law, and ought to devote every waking professional moment to being the best lawyer they can be. Under that perspective, you would be hard-pressed to show that expending time and attention toward doing programming or coding is enhancing or extending your capability to practice the law. In short, coding is far afield of lawyering and will simply dilute energies that should be solely devoted to the law.

Not to be outdone or drowned out by this seemingly persuasive argument, here is the equally vocal and ostensibly powerful claim in favor of lawyers-as-coders: The future of the law will involve automation, and any lawyer worth their salt has to face the truth that being comfortable and versed in tech is an absolute necessity for survival.

Getting into coding puts a lawyer at the forefront of the tidal wave and positions them for riding the wave and possibility standing out as a leader in the legal profession and not merely just another everyday law-only myopic lawyer.

Which argument resonates most for you?

Well, since lawyers are trained and experienced in making legal arguments, the aforementioned top-line indications showcase that there is a substantive case to be made on either side of this matter. This illuminates a crucial facet that out-of-hand dismissal of lawyers-as-coders would seem to be remiss, and likewise blindly accepting the lawyers-as-coders mantra would also seem shortsighted.

As they say, your mileage will vary, depending upon your circumstance and predilections.

Let's add some more points:

- A lawyer that codes are half-in and half-out, they are unlikely to be a good coder (producing buggy software), and they are potentially undercutting their lawyering activities.

- A lawyer that learns about coding does not need to become a coder per se and instead can leverage their gleaned grasp of coding to foster the infusion of tech into the practice of law, opening doors in their law firm for career progression or sparking them toward a LegalTech startup.

- Time spent by a lawyer to become a coder is presumably unbillable and thus a money drain rather than a money booster. Let coders code, let lawyers do lawyering.

- Law firms are increasingly striving toward adding new legal services and those lawyers into coding will best be able to strategically shape and drive those efforts, bolstering the future revenue of the firm.

- You might as well say that coders ought to become lawyers, yet another misguided mismatch, plus just as lawyers would be insulted at a programmer that thinks they overnight can be a lawyer, the same can be said of lawyers falsely assuming they can simply overnight become a coder.

- ABA stipulates that lawyers are to "keep abreast of changes in the law and its practice, including the benefits and risks associated with relevant technology, engage in continuing study and education," which lawyers-as-coders is obviously abiding by that stated requirement. End of story.

- Too many lawyers doing coding in a law firm will be a nightmare, like herding cats, and likely produce lots of straggler apps that have little rhyme nor reason all told.

- And so on.

Conclusion

A final comment is that the word "coding" is perhaps misleading, though handy as a shorthand. Lawyers that learn about the use of Machine Learning can use software packages that do not require conventional programming. In that sense, lawyers-as-coders might be better represented by stating lawyers-as-tech-savvy.

That would be more sensible but sadly is not nearly as catchy a moniker.

Note: *For supplemental materials depicting the aspects discussed in this chapter, refer to Appendix B, which contains various augmented diagrams, charts, and additional related facets of relevance.*

CHAPTER 10
AI & LAW:
AGILE AI AND LAW

Key briefing points about this essay:

- Recent efforts to speed-up AI development are being coined as using Agile AI techniques

- Software development has historically relied upon the waterfall model of development

- In the classic waterfall, each step or stage is done one at a time, possibly elongating the process

- Agile AI leverages modern agile-based development involving sprints, scrums, etc.

- The use of Agile AI for developing AI-based or AI-infused LegalTech apps is being encouraged

Introduction

One of the latest trends in the field of Artificial Intelligence (AI) involves the emergence of Agile AI.

Your first thought might be that Agile AI most certainly must refer to an AI system that is nimble, able to think on its feet, and can react quickly like a sprightly ninja. Though you could decide to call any AI that is flexible and responsive to be presumably "agile" in its capacities, please be aware that's not what the standard definition of Agile AI portends.

Perhaps with some mild disappointment, you'll likely be intrigued to know that Agile AI refers to the process of crafting AI systems and doing so via the use of what are known as agile software development methods. Purportedly unlike prior methodologies, the agile approach attempts to speed up the process of developing software and simultaneously proffers the desired hope that the speed also comes with greater alignment to the needs of those that will utilize the resulting software system.

Some of you might have heard of the much-maligned waterfall model for developing software, the precursor to the agile movement.

The waterfall model or method is classically portrayed as consisting of doing each of the major steps or stages of a system development project on a one-at-a-time basis. This usually consists of first collecting all the requirements for what the system is supposed to ultimately accomplish. Next, a detailed specification is created. Then, with the spec firmly in-hand, the software coding can get underway. There is then testing to be done and eventually if all seems satisfactory, the system can be released into production and made available to the users of the system.

A criticism of this step-by-step approach is that it stretches out tremendously the timeline and thus delays getting the software into the eager arms of the users. For large-scale systems, the requirements alone could take months and months to nail down. By the time the spec is written and approved, and the software is coded and tested, the final system could be so dated in its original needs that the resulting system is no longer relevant or misses the boat of what is currently required.

You snooze, you lose.

Well, not quite, since there was not truly any snoozing going on and instead there was a lot of behind-the-scenes machinations taking place.

Of course, those awaiting the benefits of having the software do not especially care about how the kitchen is preparing the meal. End users want results and are usually clamoring to tangibly have the software at their fingertips. Telling them that the stew is carefully being put together provides little solace amid their growling and hungry stomachs awaiting the software to be readied for use.

Agile As A Manifesto

Around the year 2001, a group of well-known software specialists promulgated what has become known as the *Agile Manifesto*. In it, they argued that there needs to be a better, faster, and more fluid way of getting software systems up and running. They essentially indicated that it would be best to do a series of short time-boxed iterations and have something relatively soon for the users, albeit not yet having all the features that would eventually be included.

These quickened mini-projects are often referred to as sprints. Common parlance in the agile rubric is to have a scrum master that is responsible for pushing forward the software or system development effort. You might be familiar with the word "scrum" as used in rugby, whereby the players are jampacked together and push mightily to try and move forward with the ball. The agile approach typically conceives of the all-told effort as a scrum and the developers are presumably brought into alignment to cohesively push ahead on getting the system going.

To recap, the waterfall model is said to be like a slowly cascading flow that goes from a seemingly laborious start to an eventual and somewhat delayed finish, while the agile framework instead offers the notion of doing things in shortened or segmented series of pieces and gradually makes its way to the entire whole. That somewhat hazily depicts things, though be forewarned it is a rather sweeping and over-generalized way to compare the two approaches.

I mention this because such a depiction, which is commonly presented, insidiously makes the waterfall model appear as foolhardy and inept, unfairly so.

The reality is that the waterfall approach can have advantages over the agile. Meanwhile, if the waterfall is poorly performed, it looks intrinsically bad and thus has gotten stigmatized accordingly. In that same vein, and rarely spoken, the agile can also falter, though the approach still to this day has that honeymoon shine and few are willing to overtly point out the pitfalls and guffaws.

In any case, the advent of Agile AI consists of exploiting the agile methodologies in the effort to craft and field AI systems. This includes the creating of AI systems for the law. The thinking is that if Agile AI can work for creating AI systems in other domains, such as the medical field, engineering, agriculture, and so on, by gosh it might as well be used when creating AI-related LegalTech systems.

In a sense, much of the AI efforts in the field of law have used Agile AI, whether they realized it or not.

This is due to the aspect that there have been very few large-scale monolithic LegalTech systems built to date, and instead, most have been incrementally constructed over time. To some degree, you could say this comports with the agile framework, even if it did not ideally align.

Advanced AI-based legal reasoning systems have primarily been constructed by researchers and in various exploratory AI labs, doing so as initial prototypes or pilot systems. Those preliminary efforts are then expanded, incrementally, versus trying to do the entire enchilada from start to finish.

For such researchers, if they don't already know about Agile AI, it would be highly recommended that they consider learning more formally about it and adopting at least the golden nuggets of the approach.

Conclusion

For the newest and large-scale ambitious efforts to craft sizeable and fully embellished AI-based LegalTech, they ought to seriously weigh whether to proceed in the waterfall style or shift toward the agile mode.

The AI won't care, but the lawyers, jurists, and other legal professionals breathlessly awaiting the systems will care, so make sure that the cookery and the kitchen are armed with the best-in-class approaches and tools, aiming to get robust AI into the grueling practice of law soonest, subject to working properly and appropriately, of course.

Note: *For supplemental materials depicting the aspects discussed in this chapter, refer to Appendix B, which contains various augmented diagrams, charts, and additional related facets of relevance.*

CHAPTER 11

AI & LAW:

LEGAL ADVICE BY NANOSECOND

Key briefing points about this article:

- Lawyers tend to charge for legal advice based on hourly work (or fractions thereof)

- ABA stipulations indicate that those lawyering fees are to abide by "reasonableness" factors

- The future of lawyering will encompass AI-based legal reasoning systems

- Those AI systems will run based on nanoseconds (one billionth of a second)

- How will lawyerly legal advice be charged when AI can do so on such fractions of time

Introduction

The famous line about time being money is one that equally applies to lawyers and the practice of law. One could readily assert that the bread and butter of being an attorney is the proffering of legal services and legal advice and that this is done to both serve the cause of justice and also to put food on the table, as it were.

Typically, a lawyer will charge by the hour.

This can be arranged to occur in fractions of an hour, such as some law offices that charge on a basis of one-tenth an hour or for every six minutes of legal effort consumed, while others use a one-sixth minimum unit of ten minutes and some use a half-hour as their lowest core unit of time.

Per the stipulation of the ABA, a lawyer is to charge a fee that entails a semblance of "reasonableness" and ought to include a mixture of several factors in ascertaining that it comports with being reasonable, and therefore, presumably, does not reflect an unreasonable charge. One of those factors as stated by the ABA is that the reasonableness is based on "the time and labor required, the novelty and difficulty of the questions involved, and the skill requisite to perform the legal service properly."

Of course, charging by the hour is not the only way to go.

There are flat fee arrangements that can be made, though this is generally a rough road to travel since it can be problematic to predetermine what makes sense to charge for a case in its totality.

You either find yourself essentially over-charging by doing a lot less legal work than originally anticipated, and possibly drawing ire from the client (despite the presumed a priori agreement to a flat fee, there can nonetheless be buyer remorse or more like enmity if it seems ultimately unbalanced), or you can potentially under-charge and are said to lose your shirt in the process because you didn't get fully compensated for your efforts.

The latter instance encompasses a lost opportunity cost too of having usurped using your legal billable acumen toward other more fruitful payment opportunities.

The headline-grabbing form of legal effort compensation consists of contingency fees.

We've all witnessed the whopping windfalls that at times can occur in legal cases involving contingency payment arrangements. Indeed, circumstances that seem nearly too good to be true are oftentimes bandied around in court as to the "reasonableness" versus "unreasonableness" and attempts after-the-fact are made to alter or adjust the compensation accordingly. A long-standing argument usually made is that the upfront core risk of not getting paid or getting a pittance is the other side of the coin that can sometimes happen to land on the side that perchance brings in the big dough.

By-and-large, though a myriad of fee arrangements can be made, it seems safe to suggest that predominantly the billable time of lawyers is done on an hourly basis (or fraction thereof) and pretty much is the standard fare and generally accepted practice for today's legal profession.

Let's assume that this per hour basis as a golden rule will continue.

Down To The Split Second In Timing

Maybe the per hour approach will inevitably turn into the per nanosecond rule-of-thumb.

How's that?

First, to clarify, a nanosecond represents one billionth of a second.

That's a quite minuscule amount of a second and certainly a quite microscopic amount of an hour's worth of time.

You might be tempted to say that it is no more than the blink of an eye, but that would actually be woefully undercutting the briefness of a nanosecond since eyeblinks are about 100 milliseconds in duration (you might recall from your metric system lessons that 100 milliseconds is 100,000,000 nanoseconds, which is a boatload of nanoseconds).

Okay, so how in the world could a lawyer charge for their legal services based on a billionth of a second, given that there is no "reasonable" way to measure your legal mental processes such that somehow your neurons and synapses generated legal advice at that infinitesimal level of thought?

The answer is that we need to shift our attention momentarily away from the preoccupation with human thought and focus instead on computational processing and the role of AI-based legal reasoning systems.

We are gradually witnessing the adoption of Artificial Intelligence (AI) into the field of law and the practice of law. This initiative will initially consist of semi-autonomous AI legal reasoning systems that are devised to work hand-in-hand with human lawyers. The AI as a legal tool will be at the fingertips of lawyers preparing for a case and provide augmented legal guidance and legal suggestions about how to proceed.

Eventually, there is bound to be created more fully autonomous AI-based legal reasoning, and thus no need for working directly with a human lawyer per se. That's to say, the AI system would be considered the equivalent of a human lawyer in terms of dispensing legal advice and can work directly in that capacity as a legal advisor. Human lawyers could certainly still interact with and utilize such AI, but this would be due to the desire to have a lawyer-to-lawyer kind of dialogue and not because the AI system is lacking in legal acumen and needs the added crutch of relying on a human attorney.

When it comes to charging for legal advice, an AI-based legal reasoning system works on the speed of computing, traditionally taking place based on nanoseconds, and it could be that a legal case can be assessed, and legal advice rendered, in that timeframe.

Would you, therefore, charge the client based on nanoseconds worth of legal advice?

Seems laughable today. Imagine the reaction of a client. What's this charge for a thousand nanoseconds doing on my bill?

Also, the question arises as to what dollar amount might be charged for AI-based legal advice. If you charge the same as the hourly rate of human lawyers, you likely won't be in business for very long, since even the largest of human lawyering rates if divided into billionths is a fraction of a fraction of a fraction of a cent.

Conclusion

Of course, some say don't worry about it now, we'll simply cross that bridge when that day arrives.

Yes, this can seemingly be postponed until then, though the odds are that whence those attorney fee struggles arise, we'll be arguing about picoseconds (one trillionth of a second) and those old-time nanoseconds will seem like snail-paced legal advice in comparison.

———————

Note: *For supplemental materials depicting the aspects discussed in this chapter, refer to Appendix B, which contains various augmented diagrams, charts, and additional related facets of relevance.*

CHAPTER 12
AI & LAW:
AI-BASED CO-COUNSEL

Key briefing points about this essay:

- It is quite common that a client might need multiple lawyers covering particular specialties

- There are rules of conduct expected of such multi-lawyering arrangements

- The future is likely to consist of AI-based legal reasoning systems that can act as a lawyer

- Those AI systems are unlikely to be a monolith and more likely to be specialized

- Thus there are important questions about the interoperability of AI-to-AI multi-lawyering

Introduction

Envision a client that is going through a divorce and there are lots of legal entanglements that need to be figured out.

The client could certainly end up with several lawyers, each bringing their particular specialty or expertise to the matters at hand. For example, a client might have a lawyer that specializes in family law while in the midst of a divorce and simultaneously have a real estate lawyer for aiding with the marital property that needs to be divvied up. We can include into this burgeoning legal team a tax lawyer and a bankruptcy lawyer, due to the client bordering on having a business that is about to go under.

One client with multiple lawyers is a rather frequent occurrence and proffers no real surprise or shock.

Coping with multiple lawyers can be complicated.

The client could be getting mixed signals from the cornucopia of attorneys and be confused about how to deal with seemingly disparate and conflicting legal advice. Meanwhile, the attorneys might also be having a rough time if they aren't used to working with each other or perhaps being kept at arm's length by the client's own demands.

In an excellent research paper published in the *University of New Hampshire Law Review* entitled "Two Lawyers, One Client, and the Duty to Communicate," the legal scholar Stephen Sieberson of the Creighton University School of Law tackles the complexities of the simpler minimum case of two lawyers for one client and stridently points out the inherent difficulties that can ensue. This core of two-at-a-time foundational instance can then be readily extrapolated when the number of lawyers involved rises to three, four, or some larger count.

Shifting gears, here's a question that might not seem patently obvious as yet.

What happens when the multiple lawyers are AI-based legal reasoning systems?

This might need some contextual background before jumping into the fray on answering the question.

There is currently underway a gradual adoption of Artificial Intelligence (AI) into the field of law and the practice of law. This effort initially consists of semi-autonomous AI legal reasoning systems that are devised to work hand-in-hand with human lawyers. The AI as a legal tool will be at the fingertips of lawyers preparing for a case and provide augmented legal guidance and legal suggestions about how to proceed.

Eventually, there is bound to be created more fully autonomous AI-based legal reasoning, and thus no need for working directly with a human lawyer per se. That's to say, the AI system would be considered the equivalent of a human lawyer in terms of dispensing legal advice and can work directly in that capacity as a legal advisor. Human lawyers could certainly still interact with and utilize such AI, but this would be due to the desire to have a lawyer-to-lawyer kind of dialogue and not because the AI system is lacking in legal acumen and needs the added crutch of relying on a human attorney.

No Monoliths Here

One aspect that might seem particularly surprising is that AI-based legal reasoning systems are unlikely to be hooked together in a gigantic cohesive legally informed knowledge base that somehow connects them entirely as a single monolith. Perhaps those wild-eyed sci-fi movies imply this kind of massive interconnectivity, but the reality is more likely to consist of relatively separate and distinct AI-based legal reasoning systems that tend to have specific specialties in their own right.

Yes, similar to how human lawyers typically focus on having a somewhat singular legal realm focus, you can expect that AI systems will be similarly domain or subdomain concentrated. There is a rather logical and straightforward explanation for why this will be so. Researchers that are crafting the AI-based legal reasoning systems are apt to try and bite off only as much as can be chewed, and as a result, dealing with specific legal realms is a lot easier than trying to take on the entire ocean, so to speak.

In essence, we are likely to initially see AI that can do well in say the area of real estate law but has no capability for any other legal areas. Some other researchers or developers might be crafting an AI system entailing family law. And so on, for which few of these efforts are being coordinated or acting in concert with each other.

In that manner, a client that might make use of fully autonomous AI-based legal reasoning systems might need to log into one that can handle family law, and then log into another that can deal with real estate, etc. A simple analogy might be dealing with having online accounts at a multitude of banks and having to shuffle around funds by logging into each of them, acting as your own aggregator or consolidator.

Of course, the banking analogy breaks down right away since the use case here involves legal advice and the need to ensure that it legally meshes together appropriately.

In short, we'll need to devise some flavor of interoperability for AI-to-AI multi-lawyering.

There will need to be a means for the disparate AI-based legal reasoning systems to connect and communicate with each other. In today's computing parlance, a standardized form of API (Application Programming Interface) will need to be devised.

But that's just the start.

Besides having interconnectivity, we would want these legal beagle AI systems to confer with each other. The expectation of human lawyers is that they would hopefully not simply toss their specialized legal words of wisdom over the transom at each other, and would instead work somewhat harmoniously for the good of the client. That same notion ought to be applied to those AI-based legal reasoning systems that would otherwise be relatively clueless about the legal realm outside their singular purview (plus, there might be a supervisory AI lawyering system that oversees the whole team).

Conclusion

Here's a final twist to this effort to harmonize.

Suppose there are potential conflicts of interest among the AI systems, and furthermore imagine that one AI system suspects that another one is operating in a manner that can legally harm the client. When such legal malfeasance is suspected, will we expect one AI to tattle on the other?

It would seem that the same trepidations and concerns of human co-counsel in multi-lawyering arrangements will undoubtedly surface in the AI-based ones. The AI ought to be bound by the same or perhaps adjusted rules of conduct and be guided by ethical expectations to ensure that justice and the client will properly be served).

––––––––––

Note: *For supplemental materials depicting the aspects discussed in this chapter, refer to Appendix B, which contains various augmented diagrams, charts, and additional related facets of relevance.*

CHAPTER 13

AI & LAW:

DEFERENTIAL BEHAVIORS IN LAW

Key briefing points about this article:

- A recent study suggests that there are adverse outcomes in courts due to deferential behavior

- Besides individual differences, there are suggested patterns across societal segments

- Many assume that AI might inevitably overcome such aspects

- It is presumed that AI-based legal reasoning systems would be unbiased and neutral

- Recent aspects about today's AI showcase inherent biases and troubling aspects that can arise

Introduction

The history of our courts carries with it the longstanding traditions of various protocols and decorum.

Some might go so far as to suggest our courts are replete with pomp and circumstance, but however expressed there is a somewhat delicate dance encompassing tradition, stipulated procedures, pecking order, and a devout semblance of exercised civility that is supposed to permeate the sanctum of the courts. Into this social milieu steps those that are steeped in the cultural norms of the courts, such as the jurists, attorneys, and other legal professionals.

Besides those infused into these norms, there are strangers afoot too.

Non-lawyers that enter into a courtroom are apt to find the environment a rather foreign experience, as though entering into a never before visited land. Where are you to stand? Where are you to sit? Can you speak at will or must you hold your tongue? A slew of questions fills the mind as the neophyte tries to cope with immersion into this otherworldly encampment.

Do all those non-lawyers entering into the esteemed courtroom habitat react and respond in the same manner?

Likely not.

Besides individual differences, there is the possibility of analyzing behaviors across segments of society and looking for potential patterns in a more collective segmentation perspective.

In his recently released book entitled "Privilege and Punishment: How Race and Class Matter in Criminal Court," Matthew Clair serving as Assistant Professor of Sociology and (by courtesy) Law at Stanford University proposes that there is an undercurrent of deferential behavior that exists and demonstrably impacts defendants in our courtrooms and judicial deliberations.

The book is based on his doctoral dissertation at Harvard University and offers a close-in look at the research that he has undertaken.

Per his dissertation, here are some key findings: "Many working-class and poor (especially those who are black) defendants in my sample exhibit a deep mistrust of their lawyers as compared with their middle-class peers. Mistrust is not simply explained by poor representation or dissatisfaction with legal outcomes; rather, mistrusting relationships are developed through at least four mostly a priori conditions: a lack of familiarity with professionals and professional expertise; cultural mismatching between attorneys and clients on the basis of racialized or classed cultural experiences and tastes; clients' perceived mistreatment by lawyers at some point in the relationship (or even prior to the relationship, given prior personal or vicarious negative experiences with other legal authorities); and, the structural inability to choose one's lawyer."

According to the study, apparently, those that lean toward being deferential tend to be middle-class and ergo appear to achieve stronger relationships with their attorney, gleaning benefits therein, while those that are less so deferential end up in a more antagonistic rapport and the resultant lawyer-client connectivity suffers. Seemingly too, this also leads to attempts of self-advocacy by those that are less deferential and produces difficulties as a result of disturbing the status quo of the court processes.

That's quite a lot to contemplate.

Shifting gears, let's consider the future of our courtrooms and how the nature of adjudication might change in an era of AI-based legal reasoning systems.

AI As Potentially Neutral Judicial Cornerstone

To clarify, there is currently underway a gradual adoption of Artificial Intelligence (AI) into the field of law and the practice of law. This effort initially consists of semi-autonomous AI legal reasoning systems that are devised to work hand-in-hand with human lawyers. The AI as a legal tool will be at the fingertips of lawyers preparing for a case and provide augmented legal guidance and legal suggestions about how to proceed.

Eventually, there is bound to be created more fully autonomous AI-based legal reasoning, and thus no need for working directly with a human lawyer per se. That's to say, the AI system would be considered the equivalent of a human lawyer in terms of dispensing legal advice and can work directly in that capacity as a legal advisor. Human lawyers could certainly still interact with and utilize such AI, but this would be due to the desire to have a lawyer-to-lawyer kind of dialogue and not because the AI system is lacking in legal acumen and needs the added crutch of relying on a human attorney.

If we are eventually going to have AI-based systems serving as lawyers and jurists, presumably this might neutralize any kind of deferential behaviors since one would likely assume that the AI will not imbue the human-to-human style interactions of today's judicial efforts. The AI conceivably treats all comers the same way.

This idealized vision though might not be so readily achieved.

One concern is that the AI will be tilted towards those that are already tech-savvy and are used to dealing with complex AI-related interactions. This implies that those that might not have had prior access to such AI systems will be at a disadvantage over others that have gotten such exposure.

Yet another qualm is whether the AI itself might contain undue biases.

We usually assume that an AI system will be entirely vacuous of any biases, but today's AI has increasingly shown that AI systems can contain biases and at times bury them so deeply that it is hard to spot them at a simple glance. Indeed, ongoing calls for XAI (explainable AI) are being raised as an important element for the acceptance of AI systems.

Blind belief in AI is not sufficient and can proffer quite undesirable outcomes.

Conclusion

In short, though AI might seem to resolve potential inequalities and injustices, the reality is that the AI that we adopt must still undergo great scrutiny and scrubbing else we might find ourselves going down dark corridors that could encompass insidious inequities and undercut the avid pursuit of justice.

———

Note: *For supplemental materials depicting the aspects discussed in this chapter, refer to Appendix B, which contains various augmented diagrams, charts, and additional related facets of relevance.*

CHAPTER 14

AI & LAW:
SLOWING AI WHEELS OF JUSTICE

Key briefing points about this essay:

- We take at face value that going faster and faster is inherently sensible and productive

- Lawyers are continually pressured to get their legal work done soonest possible

- The advent of AI-based legal reasoning systems are bound to aid that speed/time quest

- Some though question whether the speeding up of the wheels of justice is sensible

- Perhaps those AI systems will need to be slowed down to match the humanity of the law

Introduction

Speed and getting things done as quickly as possible has got to be one of the top considerations in the minds of most practicing attorneys.

Assuredly, most attorneys are constantly battling time.

There is never enough time available to get fully prepared for a case. Time slips from your fingers as you try to cover an entire stress-inducing handful of cases all at once, though none of the cases seem to get a sufficient amount of time, causing you to fret nervously over the time crunch and its repercussions.

An obvious solution to the time conundrum is to speed-up what you do. Perform your legal wizardry faster and you'll use up less time. The time saved can be repurposed toward other cases that might be time-starved or allow you to take on an even greater workload.

Faster, faster, faster, that's the mantra used by some law firms in terms of urging their partners and associates to get the job done as quickly as possible.

Of course, speed cannot come at the cost of doing a lousy job.

Espousing crummy or half-baked legal advice might seem to be a quicker way to undertake your legal services, but the odds are that doing so will ultimately have a rather dramatic and career-crushing impact.

Lawyers are required by their binding code of conduct to provide their legal wisdom thoroughly and thoughtfully. Clients aren't likely to tolerate matters if they figure out that they got the short-shrift on legal acumen because of a time-cutting or time-saving shortcut that their lawyer opted to enlist.

This focus on time and the speed or pace of legal reasoning is a notable basis for understanding how the use of Artificial Intelligence (AI) in the practice of law will potentially upend or disrupt existing legal efforts and protocols.

Efforts are underway to infuse AI into the act of legal reasoning, allowing for computer-based analyses of legal cases.

A human lawyer might confer with an AI-based legal reasoning system to provide insights about how to approach a new case. Acting as a kind of armchair legal adviser, the AI system is devised to proffer legal arguments and counterarguments, including citing related precedents and uncovering the reasoning that underlies the merits of the case.

Initially, these AI systems will be ostensibly semi-autonomous, meaning that they will only work properly if handled by a human attorney at the wheel, as it were. The hope by those in the cojoined AI-and-the-law field is that eventually these systems will be extended to become fully autonomous. In short, a fully autonomous AI-based legal reasoning system could undertake the same legal advisory role of a human attorney, doing so without any need or requirement for a human lawyer to be involved.

AI Legal Reasoning And Speed/Time

How does the advent of AI-based legal reasoning apply to the matter of time and speed?

It is sensibly presumed that a human lawyer armed with such an AI system could undoubtedly pursue a legal case much more quickly via the AI sounding-board, and thus speed-up their legal work. Indeed, the assumption is that the speeding up would be more than just dribbling and could effectively transform one human lawyer into the equivalent of several attorneys or perhaps dozens of them.

Does going faster always make sense or might speed be detrimental?

The downsides of sped-up legal efforts are judiciously discussed by legal scholar Laurence Diver of the Law, Science, Technology & Society (LSTS) research group at Vrije University in Brussels, doing so in his research paper "Computational legalism and the affordance of delay in law" (published in the *Journal of Cross-Disciplinary Research in Computational Law*, December 2020).

Per the research paper: "We should think of delay as a normative affordance that is fundamental to the nature of law-as-we-know-it, and not something that is intrinsically undesirable and always to is eliminated. The challenge is to identify those points at which it contributes to the legal practice at hand, and to translate it as necessary into the design of the computational tools that are increasingly being integrated into the legal system."

The perhaps surprising point is that our legal process and form of adjudication could be argued as shaped around the assumption that delays will occur and that ergo we cannot necessarily opt to accelerate the wheels of justice. The squeezing out of time could be tantamount to also squeezing out an essence that produces suitable justice, as suggested by the paper: "The challenge that arises, therefore, is to identify where delay actually matters in a legal system that is built around text-driven normativity (as well as where it is *un*desirable, for example in terms of facilitating access to justice). Some delays are beneficial, others are negative."

The thing is, those developing AI-based legal reasoning systems are likely to believe that finding ways to speed-up legal efforts is altogether a quite noble quest and ought to be pursued, even if those practicing law might express qualms about doing so. As such, the researcher implores: "Part of that challenge will be to convince those of a computationalist bent that efficiency is not an end in itself. In making such an assessment we have to be clear-eyed about the nature of the computational system being mooted, the point in the legal process where it will be deployed and the role in affording legality played by the 'human' task that it will replace or augment."

Should there be built-in speed brakes or other technological mechanisms intentionally interposed to slowdown AI-based legal reasoning systems?

For some, those are crazy talk words, while for others the notion makes abundant sense.

All told, an argument that some would make is that the inherent nature of the legal struggle, consisting of the practice of law and the pursuit of justice, inextricably is human-based and must move therefore at human-like speeds. Others reject this credo and emphasize that humans use a multitude of essential aids and automation to speed-up their lives, thus the law should not attempt to separate itself from these commonalities and cannot seek to holdback tech by clamoring that slowness is somehow intrinsically better.

Conclusion

Be thinking about this ongoing debate about the nature of speed in the law, and how we can find a means to avert the criticism that perhaps excessive speed undercuts justice, while at the same time embracing those insisting that they have a desire for speed since justice delayed is justice denied.

Having the feeling of a need for speed doesn't axiomatically mean that unbridled speed per se is warranted.

.

Note: *For supplemental materials depicting the aspects discussed in this chapter, refer to Appendix B, which contains various augmented diagrams, charts, and additional related facets of relevance.*

Dr. Lance B. Eliot

CHAPTER 15
AI & LAW:
DEHUMANIZING LAWYERS

Key briefing points about this essay:

- There are a lot of jokes about lawyers and for which oftentimes are quite over-the-top

- And yet people tend to relish and respect an attorney once they have a personal need for one

- The advent of AI-based legal reasoning systems could shake-up the perception of attorneys

- One expressed qualm is that AI will lead to human lawyers being treated as though automata

- Dehumanizing of attorneys and the legal profession could be a sour outcome accordingly

Introduction

Jokes are in the eye of the beholder.

I'm sure that most lawyers can take a joke as much as anyone else can. That being said, there are certainly quite a lot of rather abrasive jokes about lawyers. These allegedly funny jibes arise in movies, on TV shows, and sometimes make their way into the everyday news. For some lawyers, they let the remarks flow off their backs like a duck in water, while other attorneys find themselves weary and altogether disgusted by the tiresome ribbing.

Jokes about the cutthroat nature of lawyers are abundant and often are told with an expectation of uproarious laughter following the punch line. These "humorous" quips are often expressed with a raising of the eyebrows and a knowing wink, as though everyone realizes the veracity of the underlying witticism that stokes the wisecrack with its hilarity.

Meanwhile, when non-lawyers find themselves in need of a lawyer, things turn quite serious. The assumption is that their lawyer will in fact go to the ends of the earth to try and argue their case. Tossed to the wayside are those qualms about lawyers being overly zealous. A person employing a lawyer wants that attorney to be a powerful thunderstorm of legal lightning and thunder.

For those of you that might remember the famous comedian Rodney Dangerfield, he used to lament that he didn't get any respect (this was a running gag, popularly so). You could assert that lawyers don't get any respect, at least not until someone feels the direct pangs of needing a lawyer as their legal muscle.

Despite the wavering or oscillating levels of respect, there is nonetheless a realization that lawyers are human beings and they are fraught with the same semblance of feelings, foibles, and aspirations as the rest of us.

Some legal scholars believe that there might be a reckoning that will turn upside down the perception of lawyers as humans, rendering attorneys into becoming dehumanized.

How so?

The answer has to do with the emergence of Artificial Intelligence (AI) in the practice of law.

Let's first establish a foundation about the advent of AI and the law, and then we can take a close look at the dehumanizing claims being fostered.

Efforts are underway to infuse AI into the act of legal reasoning, allowing for computer-based analyses of legal cases. A human lawyer might confer with an AI-based legal reasoning system to provide insights about how to approach a new case. Acting as a kind of armchair legal adviser, the AI system is devised to proffer legal arguments and counterarguments, including citing related precedents and uncovering the reasoning that underlies the merits of the case.

Initially, these AI systems will be semi-autonomous, meaning that they will only work properly if handled by a human attorney at the wheel, as it were. The hope by those in the cojoined AI-and-the-law field is that eventually these systems will be extended to become fully autonomous. In short, a fully autonomous AI-based legal reasoning system could undertake the same legal advisory role of a human attorney, doing so without any need or requirement for a human lawyer to be involved.

Dehumanizing Lawyers Due To AI Lawyering

How does the advent of AI-based legal reasoning apply to the perceived dehumanization of lawyers?

Strap yourself into your seat and get ready for this legal beagle conundrum.

If the AI can ostensibly be a co-equal to human attorneys in performing legal reasoning, this might cause the general public to rethink the intrinsic nature of human lawyers. In short, if a robot can do it, this lawyering stuff must be relatively straightforward and can be presumably done by anything or anyone akin to automata.

In that manifestation, there is seemingly no notable difference between a human performing the work versus the automata performing the work. The human is no better and no worse than the automata. From there, the mental leap is that the human might as well be treated as the equivalent of automata.

Voila, dehumanization of human attorneys.

Human lawyers are nothing more than sentient objects that can perform legal work. If you extract the humanness, you've got at their core the same essence as those AI-based legal reasoning systems. Since all that someone presumably wants or needs is the lawyering aspects, the humanness is possibly superfluous or worse still is detrimental.

The semblance of respect for those that practice law would drop like a rock down a never-ending abyss. No need to be deferential to human lawyers. They are the same as a computer. You don't treat a computer with any semblance of special respect, thus the same can be done toward human lawyers.

Some prospective clients might "reason" that a computer is better in that it won't talk back and it won't get its feelings hurt. Just tell the AI what kind of legal problem you have, and it will tirelessly and without any emotional grumblings get the job done. This belief, though indubitably flawed, would nonetheless further inflate the dehumanization.

There would possibly be a widespread loss of dignity associated with being a human attorney. Whereas lawyers had been the butt of jokes due to their presumed zealousness, now they would be the punchline in any humorous anecdote about indistinguishability of automata versus human experts.

Adding more fuel to this nightmarish scenario, there would be a diluted sense of value associated with human lawyers. Gone would be the days of high-priced human attorneys. You can get legal advice for pennies on the dollar from AI, and the same pricing ought to be assigned to those equivalent human attorneys.

Okay, that's enough and I'll stop there, since you by now are probably getting the heebie-jeebies and are undoubtedly worried that the writing is on the wall of a seemingly bleak future for those in the legal profession. I sincerely hope that the preceding futuristic state-of-woe is not overly upsetting and nor discouraging to those that are just now beginning their legal careers.

Beyond the notion that the aforementioned future seems a bit outsized and outlandish, the prospects of AI-based legal reasoning of the prophesied human caliber is a faraway possibility and a quite longer-term outlook.

Conclusion

Upon further mulling over this prospective future, one supposes that if you had to choose between the abrasive jokes about lawyers as ambulance chasers versus jokes of lawyers as being no different than a toaster or a refrigerator (in terms of forms of automata), enduring the foul-tasting splays of humor about lawyers as sharks or pit bulls seems a bit more tolerable.

Well, just barely so.

———————

Note: *For supplemental materials depicting the aspects discussed in this chapter, refer to Appendix B, which contains various augmented diagrams, charts, and additional related facets of relevance.*

CHAPTER 16

AI & LAW:
GIFTING OF AI LEGAL ADVICE

Key briefing points about this essay:

- AI-based legal reasoning systems will arise as initially being semi-autonomous

- Gradually, there will be advancement toward fully autonomous versions

- It is widely assumed that such AI will be very expensive to use

- Can a law firm "gift" to the courts the use of an AI system to aid justice?

- Per an extendable interpretation of the Code of Judicial Ethics, the answer seems to be no

Introduction

Take a moment to contemplate how the use of AI-based legal reasoning systems might arise in our courts.

First, some essential background.

We are gradually witnessing the adoption of Artificial Intelligence (AI) into the field of law and the practice of law. This is initially consisting of semi-autonomous AI legal reasoning systems that are devised to work hand-in-hand with human lawyers. The AI as a legal tool will be at the fingertips of lawyers preparing for a case and provide augmented legal guidance and legal suggestions about how to proceed.

Inexorably, there is bound to be created more fully autonomous AI-based legal reasoning, and thus no need for working directly with a human lawyer per se.

That is to say, the AI system would be considered the equivalent of a human lawyer in terms of dispensing legal advice and can work directly in that capacity as a legal advisor. Human lawyers could certainly still interact with and utilize such AI, but this would be due to the desire to have a lawyer-to-lawyer kind of dialogue and not because the AI system is lacking in legal acumen and needs the added crutch of relying on a human attorney.

How much will it cost to tap into a semi-autonomous or fully autonomous AI-based legal reasoning system?

Nobody yet knows what the cost will be.

The odds are that the costs will undoubtedly be high whence this moonshot-style innovation first becomes readily available (i.e., beyond just backroom experiments or prototypes). Indeed, there are some qualms that only BigLaw will be able to afford such sophisticated systems. The touted concern is that adjudication will further be split into the have's and have not's, for which those that can afford the AI-based legal reasoning systems will have a decided advantage in their judicial activities over those that don't have the bucks to access them.

Another question arises as to whether the courts will also be using such AI capabilities.

They might want to use AI, perhaps eagerly so, but given that the courts are oftentimes strapped for funds, it would seem dubious that the courts and justices would have these advanced legal advisory systems at their fingertips. The odds are that the courts will go without, perhaps long after these AI computational legal beagles have become relatively commonplace in major law firms throughout the country.

AI Legal Advice As A Gifting Act

Imagine then the following scenario.

An appellate justice is trying to dig into a rather complicated case. There isn't sufficient legal talent of the humankind available to work on the matter. Turns out that just a few hours or perhaps even a smattering of computational minutes using an AI-based legal reasoning system could demonstratively move along the case and provide substantive insight for the judge and the court.

Along comes a law firm that has an AI system that specializes in the particular legal realm of the case being explored by the court.

The law firm has no involvement whatsoever in this particular case. In an ostensibly altruistic gesture of support for the courts and all told advancement of justice and the law, this particular law firm provides to the court a free-access pass to use the AI system. This includes a dedicated login, nearly unlimited AI computational processing time, and privacy such that whatever the court does online will be unrecorded within the system.

Purportedly, this is a no-strings-attached proffering of legal services, albeit not human-based but instead AI-based.

How does this strike you in terms of any perturbation of expected ethical conduct and the Code of Judicial Ethics?

Perhaps this resonates with your sensibilities as a no harm, no foul, or maybe instead rears an ugly semblance of being outright egregious and ought to be stopped dead in its tracks.

Shift the scenario and envision that the AI-based legal reasoning system was instead a human lawyer and this law firm was proffering the legal services of a human rather than an AI system. Per the California Supreme Court Committee on Judicial Ethics Opinions, posted February 9, 2021 (CJEO Expedited Opinion 2021-038), there was a presumably akin question addressed: "May an appellate justice ethically accept the services of an attorney, who is an employee and incoming associate of a law firm, to work in the justice's chambers for a period of six to twelve months?"

Your first thought might be that the question posed is unlike the scenario involving the AI-based legal reasoning system. For example, the AI system is not classified as an employee of the law firm (note that the notion of AI as being sentient and possessing legal personhood is rather far futuristic and not pertinent to this nearer-term envisioned scenario). The AI is not an associate of the law firm. The AI won't likely be provided for a period of six to twelve months, in the sense that the judge can likely access the AI in one or two sittings and be rather expeditiously done with the access, possibly in just a few days' time.

Do those differences make a difference?

Consider first what the CJEO said about the question of accepting the services of a human attorney as stated in the aforementioned question: "The attorney's services constitute a gift from the law firm. The code defines a gift as 'anything of value to the extent that consideration of equal or greater value is not received' and bans gifts, favors, and loans, unless an exception applies." In terms of defining the intrinsic nature of a gift, this was further stated as: "This committee has interpreted the code definition to mean that a gift is anything with market value."

One extendable interpretation of that opinion is that the AI-based legal reasoning system would be construed too as a form of a gift, which could straightforwardly be ascertained via the imputed or actual market value of utilizing such an AI system.

You might try to argue that the AI is somehow able to fit within the rules of exceptions. That might be a bit of a stretch, and furthermore, the CJEO stated in this cited human attorney instance an additional consideration: "Even if the gift was permissible under an exception, accepting the attorney's services would impermissibly lend the judiciary's prestige to benefit a private law firm."

Conclusion

Unless some other angle or posture emerges due to the peculiarities of an AI-related infusion, it seems as though loaning out the free use of an AI-based legal reasoning system from a law firm to the courts would be generally untenable.

Though, then again, once the AI legal reasoning is up and running, maybe we can ask what opinion it would render regarding such an ethical conundrum.

———————

Note: *For supplemental materials depicting the aspects discussed in this chapter, refer to Appendix B, which contains various augmented diagrams, charts, and additional related facets of relevance.*

CHAPTER 17

AI & LAW:
WHEN AI IS EVIDENTIARY

Key briefing points about this essay:

- AI and Machine Learning (ML) systems are increasingly being used throughout society

- An open-ended issue surrounds the evidentiary nature of AI and ML

- Legal scholars are in the midst of debating the admissibility aspects

- One expressed viewpoint has compared AI/ML to the famous Daubert Criteria

- In brief, these authors contend that arguments can be made for and against such admissibility

Introduction

There is AI in our future.

This is occurring in our everyday lives and inexorably entering into the law in a myriad of ways.

Consider the notion of AI being brought into court for evidentiary purposes. Your first thought might be that a walking-talking robot will brashly enter the courtroom and be sworn-in at the witness stand. Though there is certainly extensive effort afoot to create robots that look like humans, the AI we'll likely be experiencing in the near-term is bound to be online and utilized via a conventional screen and keyboard (well, more so via voice rather than tapping at conventional keys, akin to using Alexa or Siri).

Of course, depending upon your definition of AI, there is an argument to be made that AI is already serving in an evidentiary capacity.

How so?

Let's consider the points made in the recently published *2020 Handbook on AI and International Law*, put together by The Indian Society of Artificial Intelligence & Law (ISAIL). In Chapter 18, there is a fascinating portion by legal scholars Mridutpal Bhattacharya and Arundhati Kale that discusses the topic of AI and Machine Learning in the role of evidentiary mechanisms.

Before we jump into the evidentiary aspects, it might be handy to clarify something about AI.

The AI of today is not sentient.

There is quite a slim indication that we will anytime soon attain AI that is sentient. Despite all the headlines that might decry the pending moment of AI singularity, whereby the AI spontaneously becomes sentient, please know that this is puffery and will either "never" happen or will occur a long time from now (one hates to use the word "never" since that is altogether arguable, thus, I've opted to put the wording in quotes and highlight that we don't know if automata sentience is even achievable).

Meanwhile, you've abundantly been reading or hearing about Machine Learning and Deep Learning, the darlings of the AI field that have helped spark renewed interest and seemingly generated outsized expectations about what is possible to achieve with AI.

The advent of Machine Learning and Deep Learning has stoked an otherworldly impression of somehow magical powers underlying contemporary AI. Nope, there isn't any magic involved. Similar to knowing how the magician pulls a rabbit out of a hat, these AI techniques and technologies are actually utilizing computational pattern matching as a means to train on gobs of data and then produce outputs that have an appearance as though somewhat intelligently devised.

Again, no sentience underlies these machine-based actions. The computer crunches through numbers and data, providing responsiveness that can at a glance seem as human-like, though there is no foundational core such as common-sense or altogether common-sense reasoning that spurs this surface-level intelligible interaction.

With that vital preamble, now let's jump into the evidentiary waters.

AI/ML Evidentiary Admissibility

Per the aforementioned ISAIL Handbook, there are numerous existing and newly emerging applications of AI and Machine Learning in the law of evidence, including such aspects as risk assessment in parole hearings, facial recognition, body recognition, and the like. By-and-large, this AI-generated evidence is considered as a class of documentary evidence, though some are formulating arguments that AI can be construed as a form of witness testimony, a rather contentious and fervently being debated topic.

The authors point out that the use of AI is often likened to the use of DNA as a form of evidentiary tool or apparatus.

This comparison though is criticized by the researchers for its lack of being a proper analogy: "But the underlying technology behind DNA testing and that of AI-generated evidence is different, since AI is far more superior in its functioning, allowing tasks like monitoring, traceability, evaluation of human behavior and thus are able to act independently. Hence, they are usually classified as a third-generation forensic evidence."

You might be wondering what the U.S. federal law says about AI and Machine Learning as an evidentiary permissible construct.

As noted by the researchers: "Under the US federal law, machine learning output is used as a substantive evidence, and as such forms part of expert testimony under Rule 702 and the Daubert criteria. How far is it admissible in a state depends on an individual state's rules of evidence." Essential qualities associated with expert testimony are summarized as being testimony flourished to aid the trier of fact, which must be backed by sufficient facts or data, and has to be reliable and applicable to the case at hand.

The reference to the Daubert Criteria pertains to the famous 1993 case of *Daubert v. Merrell Dow Pharmaceuticals*, Inc., 509 U.S. 579, and the resultant overall framework clarified and established by the U.S. Supreme Court regarding the admissibility of expert testimony. Per that ruling: "Many considerations will bear on the inquiry, including whether the theory or technique in question can be (and has been) tested, whether it has been subjected to peer review and publication, its known or potential error rate and the existence and maintenance of standards controlling its operation, and whether it has attracted widespread acceptance within a relevant scientific community. The inquiry is a flexible one, and its focus must be solely on principles and methodology, not on the conclusions that they generate."

So, can AI and Machine Learning meet that threshold?

In short, the researchers concluded that those considerations do not *preclude* the use of AI and Machine Learning as evidentiary machinations, which implies that they can potentially be admissible.

At the same time, they closely inspect the Daubert Criteria and assert that today's AI and Machine Learning can currently be said to readily satisfy only some but not all of the factors.

Conclusion

All told, the use of AI and Machine Learning as evidentiary armament is open to debate and a potentially convincing argument has to be crafted and put forth to withstand likely objections to its use. The greyish nature means that it can potentially prevail as valid, though must first overcome a barrage of legal attacks.

Depending on whether you wish to embrace such evidentiary material or are desirous of rejecting it, and as with most matters entailing the law, a thorny and adversarial debate is likely to ensue.

.

Note: *For supplemental materials depicting the aspects discussed in this chapter, refer to Appendix B, which contains various augmented diagrams, charts, and additional related facets of relevance.*

CHAPTER 18

AI & LAW:
LEGAL MAPS

Key briefing points about this essay:

- There are plenty of map apps and online maps available these days

- Using an electronic-based map provides nifty features such as zoom-in and zoom-out

- Google Maps is the 500-pound gorilla and provides lots of added features such as data overlays

- For the law, envision a Legal Maps online system that was akin to the Google Maps aspects

- Boost the Legal Maps by also adding AI capabilities into the mix

Introduction

I'm betting that whenever you are planning a trip or are underway on one, you most likely are going to refer to an online or electronic-based geographical map.

They are immensely helpful.

Of the numerous mapping systems available, Google Maps has risen to be one of the most famous and altogether effusively popular of the revered maps apps (I'll explain in a moment why Google Maps is being singled out in this discussion).

For those of you that used to rely on paper-based maps, you might recall the difficulties associated with trying to find a particular locale on a map and also how hard it was to physically zoom-in and zoom-out in terms of street-level navigation versus city-to-city traversal. The beauty of online mapping systems is that you can instantly go to the lowest level of detail, and the next moment expand the view to see an entire town, or an entire state, or an entire country, and indeed nearly the entire globe via an outer space point-of-view.

Modern online maps provide a lot more than just a geographical portrayal.

You can oftentimes overlay other valuable data. For example, you might be wondering about population-related aspects and thus include a filter that showcases where people are living in a given city or town. Perhaps you are thinking of moving to a new place and are curious what the income levels are like in that region. With a flick of a switch or press of a button, you can display income-related data across a geographical area and add various colors or icons to illuminate the information.

Why all this talk about mapping systems?

A proposed new approach to the law has proffered the idea that there ought to be a kind of equivalent to Google Maps but instead focused on the law. This incarnation has been coined as Legal Maps.

In an innovative research article published in the Iowa Law Review entitled "Measuring, Monitoring, and Managing Legal Complexity," esteemed legal scholars J.B. Ruhl and Dan Katz propose that: "Legal Maps would be built on the same kind of platform like Google Maps, starting with layers of data relevant to the legal system network. For example, the hierarchy network of the United States

Code would be represented as a discrete layer, as would the hierarchies of the Code of Federal Regulations, the federal courts, and the corollaries for states."

Give this idea a moment to percolate in your mind.

Seems pretty handy.

Plus, the analogy to Google Maps makes the notion readily comprehensible and quite easy to communicate as to how the Legal Maps might work. You can use the same zoom-in and zoom-out functions of a geographical mapping system, though doing so via passages of text and legal artifacts.

Much of today's laws are stored in completely separate systems and trying to pin the tail on the donkey of finding or tying together related laws is an arduous and exceedingly frustrating task. Sure, there are pockets of online databases here and there that have snippets of this or that laws, but the Legal Maps concept is that you would have at your fingertips the entirety of laws, nationally and globally contained in one easy to access system.

And, don't forget the analogous idea of being able to overlay other related data. Per the researchers: "Additional layers relevant to the system behavior could be added—such as provisions of the Constitution, citations in attorney briefs, administrative rulings, and so on—and the interconnections within and between each layer could be mapped."

Another important facet of Legal Maps would be the same type of real-time instantly available access that you can get when using Google Maps. With Google Maps, you can pretty much access the mapping capabilities whenever you wish to do so, whether at the office during the day or maybe late at night when planning an upcoming trip for work or play.

That being said, we also know that Google Maps is not necessarily real-time accurate. It could be that an online map is somewhat out-of-date, perhaps having been physically mapped a week ago or a month ago. Thus, you need to be cautious to not fall into the mental trap of assuming that the online map is necessarily precisely what exists in the world at the moment that you do your inquiry.

The legal scholars make note of this real-time facet: "Legal Maps, like Google Maps, would also operate as a real-time (or nearly real-time) representation of the legal system's dynamics. Events such as promulgation or repeal of a regulation or a new judicial opinion can be streamed into the map system with appropriate representations of cross-references and citations, and the system's information flow paths and rates could be observed (e.g., are certain regulations strong gatekeeper nodes between the statutory provisions they reference and judicial opinions referencing the regulation?)."

Adding AI Into The Mix

An additional augmentation of the envisioned Legal Maps would encompass AI capabilities.

Let's take a quick side tour of AI and the law, and then come back to the Legal Maps topic.

We are gradually witnessing the adoption of Artificial Intelligence (AI) into the field of law and the practice of law. This is initially consisting of semi-autonomous AI legal reasoning systems that are devised to work hand-in-hand with human lawyers. The AI as a legal tool will be at the fingertips of lawyers preparing for a case and provide augmented legal guidance and legal suggestions about how to proceed.

Inexorably, there is bound to be created more fully autonomous AI-based legal reasoning, and thus no need for working directly with a human lawyer per se.

That is to say, the AI system would be considered the equivalent of a human lawyer in terms of dispensing legal advice and can work directly in that capacity as a legal advisor. Human lawyers could certainly still interact with and utilize such AI, but this would be due to the desire to have a lawyer-to-lawyer kind of dialogue and not because the AI system is lacking in legal acumen and needs the added crutch of relying on a human attorney.

Here's how Legal Maps might include AI capabilities: "Legal Maps could use the same machine-learning technology in the form of embedded algorithms to identify red-flag conditions of excessive legal complexity, such as synchronization and information-flow surges and blockages, the same way Google Maps shows the impacts of an interstate being shut down on surrounding roadway traffic."

Conclusion

A final twist about the use of AI would be as a means to inform lawmakers about how laws are being exercised and tested: "Over time, regulators could begin to learn from Legal Maps' learning, the way Google Maps learns about driver responses to traffic situations, gaining important perspectives about when and where legal system complexity appears to be approaching conditions of high systemic risk, as well as lessons about legal institution and instrument design that can reduce such stress."

Extending beyond those facets, envision too that as AI-based Legal Reasoning (AILR) systems progress toward being semi-autonomous and potentially autonomous, the Legal Maps capability could become infused with advanced automation that proffers readily accessible legal advisory capabilities.

Any users of Legal Maps would ostensibly have at their fingertips a versed AI-rendered "lawyer" available for immediate access, able to explore and interpret what the colossal legal database portends. This could happen in real-time and whenever so accessed.

All told, the AI amplification could enable existing attorneys to confer with the Legal Maps system on somewhat of a peer basis, and meanwhile assist non-lawyers in being aware of what they are viewing and how to appropriately comprehend what Legal Maps provides.

All of this is mainly on the drawing board, serving as a blueprint, but perhaps those of an enterprising bent will take up arms and someday bring to the legal world a full-blown splendor known as Legal Maps).

.

Note: *For supplemental materials depicting the aspects discussed in this chapter, refer to Appendix B, which contains various augmented diagrams, charts, and additional related facets of relevance.*

CHAPTER 19
AI & LAW:
POSTHUMANIZATION

Key briefing points about this essay:

- Legal personhood applies to a natural person or commonly expressed as a human being

- There is juridical personhood reserved for artificial persons

- Generally, there is a somewhat strident dichotomy of being able to differentiate those two

- A posthumanization era will portend a blurring of human versus non-human facets

- The act of "thinking" is an unlikely tiebreaker since AI will undercut that difference

Introduction

With the widespread use of today's Natural Language Processing (NLP) systems, such as the vaunted Alexa and Siri, it is becoming increasingly difficult to discern whether a computer that is speaking to you is a human or non-human.

This confusion can occur in the spoken word and also in the written word.

From a legal personhood perspective, I think it is fairly safe to say that I am a natural person, that is, I exist as a human being and in the form of a physical humanoid. Of course, you don't know for sure that my brash assertion is necessarily true since it could be that there is an AI system that has composed these words. Thus, for all you know, an artificial entity is pulling the wool over your eyes by claiming to be a natural person when in fact all of this is being produced by a non-human.

One question that immediately arises is whether a non-human artificial entity can be considered as garnering the label of "person" or personhood and whether it should be granted a formal kind of juridical personhood treatment within the law.

Throughout those types of thorny debates, there is usually an assumption that we only have to deal with two rather starkly contrasting choices, namely that someone or something is either human or they are non-human. This strident dichotomy makes the legal quandary somewhat easier since we only have to cope with the legal aspects that are going to be ascribed to the non-human and ergo ultimately decide how human-oriented legal rights might apply to this non-human thingamajig (or should that be thingamabob?).

Even if you decide to toss animals into the fray and argue that your beloved dog or favored cat should get a modicum of legal personhood, at least we would all likely agree that those wondrous creatures are non-human. Of course, technically, a human is also an animal, squarely situated within the animal kingdom, but, hey, the overarching point is that the human-animal is ostensibly the only classifiable humanoid within the totality of all animals known to mankind.

You are going to have to prepare yourself for some eyebrow-raising news.

In a so-called posthumanist era, you'll need to cast aside the simplistic binominal dichotomy and cope with fluidity or a wide spectrum of human and non-human semblance that will readily make your head spin.

In a fascinating research paper by Matthew Gladden entitled "The Diffuse Intelligent Other: An Ontology of Nonlocalizable Robots as Moral and Legal Actors" in *Social Robots: Boundaries, Potential, Challenges*, he discusses the envisioned posthumanist era this way: "We live in an era of accelerating technological posthumanization in which the form and capacities of human and artificial agents are converging in ways that might be understood as either exciting or unsettling. Ongoing developments in fields like biocybernetics, neuroprosthetics, wearable computing, virtual reality, and genetic engineering are yielding technologically augmented human beings who possess physical components and behaviors resembling those traditionally found in electronic computers."

In short, there won't be a quick-and-dirty way to instantaneously ascertain that someone or something is human versus non-human. There will be humans that are merged or infused with non-human elements. There will be non-human entities that are merged or infused into humans. This conjoining will be of such gravity that a blur will occur, and you won't especially be able to declare that the result is solely a human or solely a non-human.

Myriad of Human And Non-Human Mixtures

What kind of conjoining might take place?

The research paper provides a daunting laundry list that seems to be endless: "Such entities may include 'natural' human beings who have not been biotechnologically modified; human beings possessing neuroprosthetic implants that provide extensive sensory, motor, and cognitive enhancement; human beings whose physical structures and biological processes have been intentionally sculpted through genetic engineering; human beings who spend all of their time dwelling in virtual worlds; virtualized entities resulting from a process of 'mind uploading'; artificial general intelligences; social robots; decentralized nanorobotic swarms; artificial organic or electronic life-forms, including virtual or physical robots that evolve through processes of mutation and natural selection; sentient or sapient networks; and 'hive minds' comprising groups of diverse agents linked in such a way that they can share collective sensory experiences, emotions, and volitions."

That is quite a mouthful.

Your first thought might be that it is all a bit distracting and that the crux of being a human consists of our ability to think and reason. As long as the act of human-oriented thinking is somewhere inside a concoction, it ought to be labeled as a natural person and imbue legal personhood.

Sorry, that's not going to cut the mustard.

The field of Artificial Intelligence (AI) is fully bent on being able to craft a thinking machine, as it were, whereby the computer system exhibits the same capability of thinking as humans do. Indeed, the stretch goal consists of not just meeting the mark in terms of human intelligence. There are outsized hopes of reaching *superhuman* realms of thinking (though no one can say for sure what this "superior" formulation of thinking would consist of).

You likely know that AI is even being infused into the practice of law. There are two ways to construe this linkage, consisting of AI as applied to the law, and the other means is envisioning the law as applied to AI (this all told is yet another example of a dichotomy).

In the matter of AI as applied to the law, this initially consists of semi-autonomous AI legal reasoning systems that are devised to work hand-in-hand with human lawyers. The AI as a legal tool will be at the fingertips of lawyers preparing for a case and provide augmented legal guidance and legal suggestions about how to proceed.

Inexorably, there is bound to be created more fully autonomous AI-based legal reasoning, and thus no need for working directly with a human lawyer per se.

That is to say, the AI system would be considered the equivalent of a human lawyer in terms of dispensing legal advice and can work directly in that capacity as a legal advisor.

The other side of the AI-and-law coin is the application of our laws to the emergence of AI.

It would seem that our existing laws are not up to the task of handling the widening spectrum of what might be human versus non-human in a legal personhood manner. You cannot hang your hat on the belief that if something can think it must therefore be a human and be endowed with the legal personhood of a natural person. The legal world will need to rethink the definition of the law as it relates to the cornucopia of human-like entities that are coming down the pike.

Conclusion

In the future, perhaps your fellow law partners in your firm will be a mixture of humans and posthuman forms, or then again, this might be taking place already and you just don't know it.

————————

Note: *For supplemental materials depicting the aspects discussed in this chapter, refer to Appendix B, which contains various augmented diagrams, charts, and additional related facets of relevance.*

CHAPTER 20

AI & LAW:

AI LAW NOT COMPUTABLE

Key briefing points about this essay:

- There is abundant effort afoot to create and advance AI-based legal reasoning systems

- One vexing question is whether the law is ultimately a computable number or not

- This is a perhaps similar question posed about the field of mathematics

- Historically, the Church-Turing thesis or assertion is that mathematics is not computable per se

- Some legal scholars use the same logic and contend that law is limited in the same manner

Introduction

A fierce battle continues to take place about whether the law is subject to computability or not. In a more formalized way, some boldly assert that the law is not a computable number.

If you are into mathematics or computer science, such an assertion is of keen interest, and indeed can start a quite spirited verbal sparring that could lead to fisticuffs.

For those of you into law, perhaps the statement seems either like it is non-sensical or perhaps altogether a non-sequitur.

Let's back-up a moment to see what the fuss is all about.

There is a great deal of ongoing effort toward trying to get computers to ably perform in the field of law.

We are gradually witnessing the adoption of Artificial Intelligence (AI) into the field of law and the practice of law. This is initially consisting of semi-autonomous AI legal reasoning systems that are devised to work hand-in-hand with human lawyers. The AI as a legal tool will be at the fingertips of lawyers preparing for a case and provide augmented legal guidance and legal suggestions about how to proceed.

Inexorably, there is bound to be created more fully autonomous AI-based legal reasoning, and thus no need for working directly with a human lawyer per se.

That is to say, the AI system would be considered the equivalent of a human lawyer in terms of dispensing legal advice and can work directly in that capacity as a legal advisor. Human lawyers could certainly still interact with and utilize such AI, but this would be due to the desire to have a lawyer-to-lawyer kind of dialogue and not because the AI system is lacking in legal acumen and needs the added crutch of relying on a human attorney.

A looming and overarching question is whether it will be feasible to incorporate the law into computer systems. To clarify, this is not simply embodying the text of laws, which is relatively easy to toss into online databases and instead entails the act of interpreting laws and performing AI-based legal reasoning.

In short, is the law ultimately computable or not?

Digging Into The Computability Question

A fascinating article on this topic is entitled "On computer numbers with an application to the AlanTuringproblem" and appears in the prominent journal *Artificial Intelligence and Law*. Written by legal scholars Catrin Huws and James Finnis, they posit this general belief that exists among researchers: "Instinctively, the law is something that ought to be computable, in that it ought to be possible to convert the processes of legal decision-making into an algorithm—a set of simple instructions and decisions—and thus render it computable."

Yes, intuitively, we all likely believe in our heart of hearts that the law ought to be considered computable. Maybe we haven't gotten there as yet, nonetheless, the ultimate endpoint will showcase that indeed the law is amenable to being computable such that AI-based legal reasoning will in fact arise. That is the enduring and endearing assumption of today.

Let's take a short side tangent that relates to this vexing question.

A somewhat similar question has been posed about mathematics, namely whether mathematics can be subject to computability. Your first thought might be that of course mathematics has to be entirely computable. That seems like an easy question.

Or maybe it isn't quite so easy.

As pointed out in the research article by Huws and Finnis: "In the early twentieth century, mathematics was in the throes of a 'foundational crisis'. Mathematicians of the 'formalist' school (led by David Hilbert) believed that mathematics could ultimately be reduced to a set of mechanical rules by developing a 'formal system' within which all mathematical statements could be stated."

This open question or problem is typically referred to as the *Entscheidungsproblem* (you can mention this to your mathematics friends, and they will assuredly be impressed that you know of it).

Perhaps you can also detect a bit of an analogous parallel to the open question about the field of law as being computable and, for which, some suggest that a foundational crisis currently confronts the legal profession accordingly.

What happened to the mathematics computability question, you might be wondering?

As stated in the research paper: "In 1936, two independent papers by Alan Turing and the American mathematician Alonzo Church removed the last plank of the Hilbert program by demonstrating that within a formal system as defined above, there can be no general algorithm for the determination of truth (i.e. derivability) of a statement."

In brief, this is nowadays commonly known as the Church-Turing thesis or assertion, based on a commingling of their attack or analysis of the problem. In highlighting the work by Alan Turing, the legal scholars state that: "Turing, in showing that there could be no solution to the *Entscheidungsproblem*, demonstrated that it was impossible to devise an algorithm that would indicate whether a mathematical statement was provable from a set of axioms given a set of rules—in essence, whether it was true or false, given it had total knowledge within its domain. "

Yikes, this is somewhat dismaying.

Here's the skinny.

If you believe that mathematics is not ultimately computable, you are likely going to experience a humongous uphill battle to try and argue that the law is somehow computable. In essence, you can lay onto the backs of the law-as-computability question the same or similar logic of demonstrating that mathematics is not computable, ergo, one might be tempted to conclude that the law is also not computable.

These legal scholars seem to make an ostensibly convincing case to cause some to potentially decide to toss in the towel on this matter: "If the law is a formal system—that is, if a legal decision can be arrived at by processing a given a set of axioms (the facts of a case) with a set of rules for their manipulation—then the law is subject to the *Entscheidungsproblem*."

And, adding fuel to that fire: "If the law is not a formal system (because the information required or the processing rules cannot be enumerated), then there can also be no decision process, and again we cannot predict the decision by algorithmic means."

All told whether the law is a formal system or perhaps not a formal system, either way, they conclude this: "Law is not a computable number. The law's *Entscheidungsproblem* cannot be solved. The Alan Turing Problem explains it."

Sadness ensues.

Conclusion

Not everyone is convinced of this claim and the matter remains unresolved. For those of you toiling away on devising AI-based legal reasoning, do not give up your hopes and dreams.

The day that AI-based legal reasoning is working and actively participating in the law, you can look back and proclaim that despite prior misgivings and gloomy predictions, it turns out that the law was indeed computable though perhaps in a meaning unlike that of earlier definitions.

Note: *For supplemental materials depicting the aspects discussed in this chapter, refer to Appendix B, which contains various augmented diagrams, charts, and additional related facets of relevance.*

CHAPTER 21

AI & LAW:

COLLECTIVE INTELLIGENCE

Key briefing points about this essay:

- There is a field of study known as "collective intelligence"

- When intelligence is collectively utilized, there is a chance of the sum being more than the parts

- AI is gradually embodying human intelligence and can aid the collective intelligence pursuits

- Envision too that AI will be operating in the legal field

- This gives rise to exploring a future of AI-based collective intelligence in the law

Introduction

Suppose I told you that "2 + 2 = 4" and then upped the ante by claiming that "2 + 2 = 5" and asked you to give that some thought.

Perhaps you would realize that I was trying to evoke the famous saying that the sum is greater than the parts.

Or, for those of you that don't like that particular variant of wording on this sage advice (some suggest that the given phrasing is appallingly curt and not immediately radiant), an alternative version is that the whole is greater than the sum.

No matter which way you say it, this indubitably is everyday wisdom that we all seem to have grown-up with and accept as a truism at face value. The patently apparent meaning is that if you combine together the subcomponents of something, the resulting amalgamation in its totality can produce a significantly outsized effect that otherwise individually could not be attained.

This pearl or prized gem of thought is typically attributed to Aristotle.

A debate has ensued whether Aristotle deserves such credit since it seems likely that similar insights have long existed throughout the history of humanity. Plus, the presumed indication of Aristotle that seems to give rise to the discernment is arguably not of the same meaning per se: "In the case of all things which have several parts and in which the totality is not, as it were, a mere heap, but the whole is something besides the parts, there is a cause; for even in bodies contact is the cause of unity in some cases and in others viscosity or some other such quality."

Depending upon how you wish to interpret those translated words of Aristotle, you could insist that the meaning provides only a backhanded poke at the idea of the sum being greater than the parts. Perhaps what Aristotle was identifying is that the sum might be *different* than the collected set of distinguishable parts, and he was merely attempting to explain why that might be, rather than outright declaring that the sum or whole must be of necessity "greater than" the parts themselves.

Finicky reading, you might be thinking.

Maybe so, but for most lawyers, there is some insidious delight in being able to dig into the wording of things, similar to trying to interpret the latest legislative statutes, and discover a multitude of interpretations. This is especially advantageous if an interpretation can be found that will successfully win a legal case.

Speaking of backing into a topic, the aforementioned discussion brings up the notion of collective intelligence.

Collective Intelligence And The Significance Therein

Yes, it turns out that there is an entire field of study devoted to the matter of collective intelligence.

In short, collective intelligence is the notion that we can potentially combine individual bits of intelligence and the resulting sum or whole will be greater than the parts, as it were. The additive impact of one intelligence plus the intelligence of another person can produce insights that neither alone might have gleaned.

This is undoubtedly exhibited in your law practice on a daily basis.

When trying to resolve a thorny legal case, you bring together several colleagues and with those carefully chosen razor-sharp attorneys, you are able to collectively figure out the best way to proceed. Had you asked each of them to separately try to solve the legal problem, perhaps only lesser answers would have surfaced. It was the collective intelligence that did the trick.

In an interesting research paper by Tanja Aitamurto entitled "Collective Intelligence in Law Reforms: When the Logic of the Crowds and the Logic of Policymaking Collide" and presented at the 49th Hawaii International Conference on System Sciences, the definition of collective intelligence is expressed this way: "Collective intelligence is defined here as wisdom, talent, information and knowledge that emerges in certain online circumstances and can be channeled for problem-solving." The focus of the paper is about online forms of collective intelligence; thus, the definition overtly mentions the word "online," but the nature of collective intelligence can equally arise when people are simply gathered together in-person and sharing directly their intelligence (absent of any online aspects).

The research study examined two specific virtues or presumed positives about collective intelligence, namely the role of cognitive diversity and the role of large-sized crowds.

We might intuitively assume that the more pronounced the cognitive diversity the greater the whole becomes, and likewise the larger the crowd of participants the greater the whole becomes. Upon some reflective thought, this is not necessarily the result in all instances and there can be downsides that will emerge. One supposes that sometimes there is a chance that "2 + 2 = 3" can occur when an abundance of intelligence comes together.

How can we bring together a multitude of bits of intelligence to see if a collective intelligence will produce substantive benefits?

One answer is via the use of Artificial Intelligence (AI).

AI involves embedding intelligence into computer systems, and the hope is that mankind will consequently be able to dramatically foster collective intelligence possibilities.

Furthermore, imagine bringing together a collective intelligence on a grand scale in the realm of the law and the practice of law, which could be feasible whence AI becomes further advanced.

We are gradually witnessing the adoption of Artificial Intelligence (AI) into the field of law. This is initially consisting of semi-autonomous AI legal reasoning systems that are devised to work hand-in-hand with human lawyers. The AI as a legal tool will be at the fingertips of lawyers preparing for a case and provide augmented legal guidance and legal suggestions about how to proceed.

Inexorably, there is bound to be created more fully autonomous AI-based legal reasoning, and thus no need for working directly with a human lawyer per se.

That is to say, the AI system would be considered the equivalent of a human lawyer in terms of dispensing legal advice and can work directly in that capacity as a legal advisor.

Here's a seemingly mind-bending scenario.

Suppose that AI-based legal reasoning systems are devised for each individual nation. Those nation-focused legal reasoning systems are brought together as a form of collective intelligence that could derive international and globally improved laws.

This could potentially happen on a massive scale, which would otherwise be unimaginable if trying to do the same with humans per se (even if doing so online). We might also discover new insights about the law that would enhance global activities and be used to enhance the laws and practices of the nations themselves.

Conclusion

Of course, we have to be somewhat grounded and realistic, taking into account that collective intelligence does not axiomatically mean that the sum is greater than the parts. Regrettably, we might discover a drawback that the whole is worse than the parts, generating a legal morass and legal abyss of dismal proportions.

Maybe you've experienced the same in your law practice when having brought together a gaggle of lawyers that you assumed would intrinsically produce a grand result and all you got was some disheartening legal bickering and chaos.

Regarding the future, and as a piece of *intelligent advice*, perhaps all of us should be on the watch for what collective intelligence can and cannot do.

Note: *For supplemental materials depicting the aspects discussed in this chapter, refer to Appendix B, which contains various augmented diagrams, charts, and additional related facets of relevance.*

CHAPTER 22

AI & LAW:

LIMITS OF HUMAN MIND

Key briefing points about this article:

- The human brain weighs about 3 pounds and presumably is duly constrained in its size

- Some argue that our "minds" have used the entirety of the brain and we are at our limits

- Such an argument was made about the field of mathematics and might apply to the law too

- But efforts to formulate AI-based legal reasoning might take us to the next level

- And AI might advance legal reasoning, even if the human mind remains constrained

Introduction

You come across a pile of rocks. They weigh about twenty pounds. A satchel that you are carrying can only accommodate ten pounds of rocks. You are having a bad day and face a quite puzzling quandary about what to do. As the judicious old saying goes, you cannot put twenty pounds of rocks into a ten-pound sack.

That darned satchel is just not big enough to handle the chore at hand.

Rather than focusing on rocks, let's shift gears and consider the practice of law (I realize that seems like a rather odd jump between topics, but you'll see why in a moment).

Attorneys would undoubtedly concur that the practice of law is a mindful task that requires honed cognitive skills. You need to sufficiently understand the law and be able to dutifully employ legal reasoning. Some are perhaps better at this than others, and assuredly novice lawyers are generally less mentally powerful at the law than their more seasoned partners.

Estimates suggest that the human brain contains around 100 billion neurons and perhaps 100 trillion interconnections via an intricate web of neural synapses. The brain must be pretty important because it consumes around 20% of the total body energy budget, and yet is only a minuscule 2% of the mass of the human body. On average, an adult brain weighs about 3 pounds. I think that you already know what the general size of the brain might be (if you are unsure, look in the mirror and imagine your own brain, floating gingerly inside your noggin).

Here's where the sage wisdom about the rocks comes to the fore.

When will we have reached the edge of our mental acumen as bounded by the physical size and boundaries of the brain sitting inside our heads?

In short, suppose the practice of law has nearly already reached the capacity of what our minds can achieve vis-à-vis the limits of our minds and our brains. It could be that we won't make any further substantive progress such that ostensibly the manner of how we do legal reasoning today is going to be relatively the same now as it will be in fifty years, or one hundred years, or forever.

Our minds can handle just ten pounds of legal issues (rocks) and we'll always <u>only</u> be able to carry those ten pounds, regardless of if we find ourselves faced with twenty pounds of legal wrangling.

Some might shrug their shoulders and say c'est la vie, namely, this is not a big deal to crow about and we can all rest easy and be perfectly fine with that somewhat dowdy fate. Others would decry this possibility of unimaginably already having reached the pinnacle of our mental limits for the practice of law. They anxiously holdout the hope that we will increasingly and substantively increase our legal skills and stridently advance the strenuous act of legal reasoning. The dream is that legal reasoners of the future will look back at what we were doing today and will realize how primitive we once were.

To mull over this conundrum, let's consider something of a similar worry that has arisen in the field of mathematics.

Herbert Robbins was a famous mathematician, known as a pioneering statistician, and he made a rather interesting statement in 1988 about the future of mathematics, doing so by first making an analogy to the act of running: "Nobody is going to run 100-meters in five seconds, no matter how much is invested in training and machines." He continued: "I think we've gone about as far as we can go (maybe someone can shave half a second or so from the record) unless we mutate into a strikingly different breed."

Here is the controversial logical leap that he then proffered from that foundation, outstretching to the future of mathematics and mathematical reasoning: "The same can be said about using the brain. The human mind is no different now from what it was five thousand years ago. And when it comes to mathematics, you must realize that this is the human mind at an extreme limit of its capacity."

The interpretation was that we have reached the satchel capacity when it comes to the field of mathematics. Those remarks sparked infighting that still reverberates today. Are we truly at the furthermost corners of our capacity to reason about mathematics? Will we make no substantive progress in mathematics other than a piddling of altogether insignificant stepwise advances?

Some would argue that developments in mathematics after the infamous 1980s proclamation are a sure sign that the notorious assertion was mistaken, while others contend that there is nothing to write home about as a modern-day lineage of mathematical breakthroughs that prove the claim to be undisputedly false.

AI To The Potential Rescue

Hold on, maybe there is a means to overcome the problem by getting another satchel, so to speak. Specifically, one argument is that AI is going to allow us to transcend the human brain-mind limitation (assuming that you believe that such a constraint even exists).

Perhaps this applies to attorneys too.

You likely know that AI is being infused into the practice of law. This initially consists of semi-autonomous AI legal reasoning systems that are devised to work hand-in-hand with human lawyers. The AI as a legal tool will be at the fingertips of lawyers preparing for a case and provide augmented legal guidance and legal suggestions about how to proceed.

Eventually, there is bound to be created more fully autonomous AI-based legal reasoning, and thus no need for working directly with a human lawyer per se. That is to say, the AI system would be considered the equivalent of a human lawyer in terms of dispensing legal advice and can work directly in that capacity as a legal advisor.

It could be that the emergence of AI-based autonomous legal reasoning will reveal new ways of how to think about the law and advance considerably the practice of law. Human attorneys might be able to expand their minds, despite still only having the three pounds of mass for their brains, and find themselves making giant leaps forward in human-capable legal reasoning, all as a result of devising AI that can practice the law.

Conclusion

On the other hand, maybe the AI will only be as good as humans at legal reasoning, and we can righteously conclude that humans did indeed reach their pinnacle. Well, one supposes, it could also only mean that we merely made the AI in our own image and failed to try and achieve an outstretch goal.

You'll need to make up your mind about that..

———

Note: *For supplemental materials depicting the aspects discussed in this chapter, refer to Appendix B, which contains various augmented diagrams, charts, and additional related facets of relevance.*

CHAPTER 23

AI & LAW:
JUDICIAL MACHINE READABILITY

Key briefing points about this essay:

- Judicial opinions can be tough to figure out and the writing style is often obtuse

- There have been ongoing calls for judges and courts to write in a more human-readable way

- More recently, there are calls for judicial decisions to be made readily machine-readable

- Part of the basis for wanting machine readability would be to aid AI-based legal reasoning

- Whether judicial decisions will change in style and wording seems like an uphill battle

Introduction

I'm sure that you've at one point or another tried to get a toddler to eat the right kinds of foods, or at least you've seen comedy sketches on TV and in movies that portray the challenges involved.

One approach involves spoon-feeding the child, but this can be heart-wrenching if the youngster decides to dearly resist and opts to desperately spit out those undesirable and yet quite healthy carrots and peas.

You can use your wits and seek to cajole the toddler into believing that consuming the so-called "good for you" food will make them grow up to be big and strong. And yet another avenue consists of showing them that another toddler loves to eat such nourishment, thus getting the child to then acquiesce because of peer pressure or by an innate desire to be on par with a fellow kid.

Any of those approaches might do the trick.

Or none of them will attain your sought-after goal.

In some ways, this dilemma can be likened to the law and the writing of judicial opinions.

How so?

First, you need to know that not all judicial decisions are written as stellar best sellers that deserve a Nobel Prize in literature. I think we already pretty much know this to be true, which becomes readily apparent after having lost your way in one legal opinion after another. Sometimes, the logical progression is non-existent. In other cases, there is a carefully laid out indication of the logical underpinnings, and then suddenly out-of-the-blue a mighty jump is made, leaving a gap or legal logic chasm that is vexing and altogether exasperating.

A counterargument often made is that judicial opinions are not supposed to be easy to read and nor written for the reading level of a two-year-old. Judicial decisions are carved from meaty material and therefore by their inherent nature will be relatively arcane, densely packed, and require a full heads-down no-interruptions legal focus to properly grasp. If you don't like how a legal opinion is written, this is on your shoulders, not the judges that wrote it. Pick-up your legal game and you'll have an easier time of divining the legal poetry that resides within those vaunted and revered judicial writings.

The crux of how this relates to the youngster eating healthier foods is that some earnestly believe and advocate that judicial decisions ought to be written in substantively more readable ways.

One basis for this argument is that judicial opinions could be dutifully written in a manner to enhance human readability aspects.

An interesting study utilized a tongue-in-cheek named metric that has serious uses, namely the Simple Measure of Gobbledygook (SMOG) metric, and analyzed Supreme Court opinions to assess sentence sizes and the frequency of multisyllabic wording: "Writing is central to the law. This brief essay has demonstrated some trends within Supreme Court writing styles, exploring how Supreme Court Justices' writing styles have changed as a whole over time, over individual Justice's careers, and how styles vary between Justices. We have seen that Supreme Court opinions have grown more difficult to read in recent decades, with a particular spike since 2000" (published in *The Yale Law Journal*, entitled "Judicial Gobbledygook: The Readability of Supreme Court Writing" by Ryan Whalen).

Among the thousands of Supreme Court opinions examined, the research study noted an intriguing revelation about Justice Scalia: "Although Justice Scalia has the highest SMOG score observed and a higher than average median readability, suggesting that his opinions are not easy to read, he is well-known for his strong and distinctive writing style, and he has written extensively on effective legal communication." This leads to the crucial point that the law intrinsically is likely to require a writing style that will inevitably produce high SMOG ratings, but this ought to not allow headstrong obtuse writing to become unchallenged: "While some degree of gobbledygook may be necessary in legal writing, we do not want judicial opinions to become so complex as to require SMOG warnings."

Machine Readability Intentions

Set aside human readability and consider the need for machine readability.

To clarify, the hope is that Artificial Intelligence (AI) can increasingly be infused into the practice of law. This initially consists of semi-autonomous AI legal reasoning systems that are devised to work hand-in-hand with human lawyers. The AI as a legal tool will be at the fingertips of lawyers preparing for a case and provide augmented legal guidance. Eventually, there is bound to be created more fully autonomous AI-based legal reasoning, and thus no need for working directly with a human lawyer per se. That is to say, the AI system would be considered the equivalent of a human lawyer in terms of dispensing legal advice and can work directly in that capacity as a legal advisor.

Trying to feed judicial opinions into budding AI-based legal reasoning systems and derive the meaning of those human judicial renderings is a daunting task. Some urge that the courts should write opinions with the aim of ensuring the writing is readily machine-readable and potentially amendable to computability.

Per a study by legal scholars Jameson Dempsey and Gabriel Teninbaum, they emphasize a similar refrain: "However, because judicial decisions come in many forms and styles, it is up to lawyers and courts to tease out essential elements of past decisions: e.g., holdings, tests, relative weights of factors. In this essay, we argue that judges should write opinions in anticipation of later machine processing and that in doing so they can increase the efficiency and predictability of the legal system" (paper posted in the *MIT Computational Law Report* and entitled "May it Please the Bot?").

A potential adverse consequence of trying to force stricter writing standards for machine readability could be that legally eloquent and everlasting memorable prose will no longer be utilized. As stated by Dempsey and Teninbaum: "The narrative form of decision-making has been a tradition of American courts since the nation's founding (and, before that, an important part of English judicial opinion-writing). In many instances, the language of judges is nothing less than prose, with famous lines from decisions serving as inspiration for the society they govern. This aspect of our legal culture, a broader cultural context, may be lost by the adoption of some of the more restrictive formats of writing that have been proposed in this article."

Conclusion

There is an open question about whether clearer writing necessarily implies a greater semblance of overall health and attainment in the pursuit of justice. Some assert that if AI-based legal reasoning cannot glean what it needs from the existing approach to judicial opinions, warts and all, this ought to be on the shoulders of the AI and not be pushed back into the laps of the judges and the courts.

Perhaps the desire for improvements in human readability and for reshaping to enable machine readability is not the "good foods" dietary aspiration that we need to attain. Judicial decisions might have to be accepted as they are, including the saturated fats and gobs of salt, and that's all there is to it.

.

Note: *For supplemental materials depicting the aspects discussed in this chapter, refer to Appendix B, which contains various augmented diagrams, charts, and additional related facets of relevance.*

CHAPTER 24

AI & LAW:

LEGAL ECOSYSTEM

Key briefing points about this essay:

- Ecosystems are complex and involve complicated intricacies

- Yellowstone National Park provides an exemplar of biological ecosystem complexities

- Analogously, the law and practice of law can be viewed as the legal ecosystem

- When a change is made to one part of the legal ecosystem this can induce cascading impacts

- It will be important for AI to be considered as a novel change across the entire legal ecosystem

Introduction

Biological ecosystems are oftentimes quite complex. Aspects of the ecosystem are intricately linked to other aspects. Making a change to one element can have dramatic cascading impacts.

Let's utilize an easy-to-grasp example, namely the reintroduction of wolves into the Yellowstone National Park, and then see how this might apply to the law and the practice of law. For those of you that haven't yet gone there, you really ought to include Yellowstone National Park on your vacation to-do list. This famed wilderness destination is predominantly in Wyoming, though parts extend into Montana and Idaho too, and constitutes a spectacular array of biodiversity and teeming biomes.

Do you like lush forests that seem nearly endless?

Do you enjoy expansive canyons, dramatic alpine rivers, and bubbling hot springs?

Those breathtaking recreational opportunities abound. And, although a bit touristy, there is the gushing geyser known as Old Faithful (yes, you have to go see it, since you would otherwise eventually arrive home and be roundly chastised for not having witnessed this ever-popular spectacle).

Besides the rich landscape, abundant plant life, and all of those majestic trees, you should also be aware that there are wild bears, wild bison, wild elk, and other wild creatures including wild wolves. I realize that the word "wild" was repetitively used in my depiction, but that was intentional. People that visit this vast wilderness are somehow at times under the impression that the animals therein are domesticated and tamed. Please do not fall into that mental trap. This is by-and-large a place for wild animals to roam freely and do as wild animals do.

Okay, this sets the stage for a fascinating tale about what happened when wolves were reintroduced into the Yellowstone National Park ecosystem.

It turns out that wolves in Yellowstone had been pretty much hunted out of existence by humans. Some would construe this as a good thing due to the assumption that wolves are inherently bad and ought to be nixed from the wilderness.

All it takes is for a YouTube video to showcase a wolf that takes down a stately elk, and the emotional heartbreak instills a deep-rooted desire to get rid of those evildoer predatory wolves.

When you remove a major element of an ecosystem, it can have a profound effect.

Getting rid of the wolves was not simply an act of isolation. The rest of the ecosystem adjusted accordingly, doing so in ways that turned out to worsen the conditions of Yellowstone. For example, the lack of wolves made life a lot easier for the elks. The elks then multiplied by leaps and bounds (well, okay, that's a bit of a pun), and they consumed at will the available willows and other related plants.

Meanwhile, the beavers needed those willows to survive during the harsh winters, but the elk used up the willows, leaving the beavers to essentially starve. The beaver population waned. Keep in mind though that the beavers make dams, which allow for ponds and the multiplier effects of stream hydrology to occur (where water flows throughout the wilderness). Dramatic adverse impacts arose to the stinted channeling of water and thus dealt a hefty blow to the fish. Plus, the birds that rely upon a watery landscape and the richness of fish were adversely affected too.

On and on the cascading results emerged, all due to a thinning of the wolves.

By the mid-1990s, there was only one beaver colony remaining. A decision was made by trained wildlife ecologists to reintroduce wolves as part of a newly launched Yellowstone Wolf Project. Subsequently, there are now over nine beaver colonies, the elk are kept in check, the waters are flowing again, and the ecosystem has recalibrated to once again flourishing.

Hopefully, this Yellowstone story proffers sufficient evidence to you that ecosystems have complex interdependencies, and it is rather myopic to assume otherwise. Any of us can easily fail to take this intricacy into account when making ecosystem changes.

I would assert that the same can be said for the legal ecosystem.

Legal scholars emphasize the importance of conceptualizing the law and the practice of law as a complex ecosystem, commonly referred to as the *legal ecosystem*. When contemplating changes to our judicial processes and manner and mores of adjudication, it is easy to think only about making seemingly singular "isolated" changes, and not adequately anticipate a plethora of cascading results thereupon.

In a fascinating article published in the Iowa Law Review entitled "Measuring, Monitoring, and Managing Legal Complexity," venerated legal scholars J.B. Ruhl and Dan Katz state that: "Law itself is a complex adaptive system, and it necessarily influences and is influenced by the systems it is intended to regulate or manage. Hence, a principal concern of legal theorists interested in legal complexity has been to develop some sense of how best to respond to the legal system's complexity, considering that the legal system is just one member of a system of systems."

Akin to my tale about Yellowstone, their research also leverages the everyday notion of biological ecosystems to illuminate the facets of the legal ecosystem: "One consequence of understanding the "system of systems" nature of legal regimes is the appreciation that tinkering may open up a huge can of worms. Thinking by analogy, consider what can happen in a biological ecosystem if a nonnative species is introduced, as humans have often done for what were believed to be good reasons. Often the species does not survive. Sometimes, though, the introduced species takes hold in its new environment and all chaos breaks loose. The lesson is that intervening in a complex adaptive system is a risky venture."

AI And The Legal Ecosystem

You might be wondering, what upcoming change might upend the legal ecosystem?

The introduction of Artificial Intelligence (AI) into the law.

This is initially consisting of semi-autonomous AI legal reasoning systems that are devised to work hand-in-hand with human lawyers. The AI as a legal tool will be at the fingertips of lawyers preparing for a case and provide augmented legal guidance and legal suggestions about how to proceed. Eventually, there is bound to be created more fully autonomous AI-based legal reasoning, and thus no need for working directly with a human lawyer per se. That is to say, the AI system would be considered the equivalent of a human lawyer.

AI is going to have a dramatic impact across all facets of the legal ecosystem.

A mental mistake consists of focusing only on singular and isolated impacts that might arise. For example, some pundits examine only how attorneys and their work might change. Others look only at the impacts on judges. And some analysts examine solely how the public might be impacted. Rarely is there a comprehensive look at the vastness and intricacies of interdependencies that will all adjust and readjust as AI takes hold, ergo rippling throughout the entirety of our judiciary.

Conclusion

Let's make sure that we adopt a comprehensive legal ecosystem perspective on these matters.

Perhaps you can contemplate this profound matter while watching the breathtaking sunrise across the canyons of Yellowstone, or even while in a childlike trance when witnessing Old Faithful do its tomfoolery. We can assuredly be inspired by other ecosystems to make sure that the legal ecosystem evolves fruitfully.

Note: *For supplemental materials depicting the aspects discussed in this chapter, refer to Appendix B, which contains various augmented diagrams, charts, and additional related facets of relevance.*

CHAPTER 25

AI & LAW:
OXFORD ON AUTONOMOUS LEVELS

This is a variation of a piece that was originally published by Oxford University via their School of Business Law in their online blog.

Key briefing points about this essay:

- Not all AI systems are the same in the sense of achieving autonomy (some less so, some more so)

- There are various level of autonomy that have been devised for autonomous vehicles

- Those levels can be adjusted and applied to AI legal reasoning

- A proposed set of levels of autonomy for AI legal reasoning are proffered herein

- The levels would be quite useful for legal scholars, academics and for attorneys and other practitioners in the field of law

Introduction

Ongoing attempts to infuse Artificial Intelligence (AI) into the practice of law are actively taking place by commercial vendors of LegalTech products and by legal scholars in academic research labs.

A dizzying array of new AI-enabled legal systems and state-of-the-art prototypes are oftentimes touted to the public but trying to discern the wheat from the chaff is arduous and overly problematic.

Questions arise such as how much intelligent-like behavior has been achieved and whether the latest system is an improvement over prior instances, plus if so, what is the magnitude of the advancement so incurred. Usually, the wordy narratives conveying the added features and functions are chockful of technological buzzwords and fail to sufficiently indicate the actual caliber or degree of advancement.

A key reason for this difficulty is due to ambiguities of the AI moniker per se, proffering a rather broad and vague umbrella term that is ostensibly amorphous, lacking in any substantive demarcation of what the advanced automation constitutes.

What is needed to rectify this ambiguity is a type of numeric Richter scale that denotes the level of AI that has been infused into a legal system.

As such, having a definitive and standardized set of Levels of Autonomy (LoA) for AI-powered legal reasoning systems would usefully and succinctly provide a rigorous means to denote the inured capabilities. In short, the everyday use of a universal scale would demonstrably aid in unravelling and rationalizing the claims made by LegalTech vendors, doing so to achieve a no-malarkey indication of what the latest wares forthrightly achieve.

My proposed LoA identifies seven core levels of autonomy that have been applied to AI in the law for legal reasoning capacities. The set is based upon an analogous and established standard that is used similarly for demarking the levels of autonomy for self-driving cars.

Doing so leverages lessons learned about how to best differentiate AI autonomy and provides a substantive foundation for suitably recasting into the realm of AI and the law.

Here are the seven proposed levels of autonomy associated with AI and the law:

- Level 0: No Automation for AI Legal Reasoning
- Level 1: Simple Assistance Automation for AI Legal Reasoning
- Level 2: Advanced Assistance Automation for AI Legal Reasoning
- Level 3: Semi-Autonomous Automation for AI Legal Reasoning
- Level 4: Domain Autonomous for AI Legal Reasoning
- Level 5: Fully Autonomous for AI Legal Reasoning
- Level 6: Superhuman Autonomous for AI Legal Reasoning

Consider two brief examples of how this scale can be advantageously utilized.

A vendor comes out with a boosted e-Discovery tool that claims to have Natural Language Processing (NLP) and utilizes Machine Learning, which seems impressive.

But what level does this attain?

Envision that upon the appropriate rating, the e-Discovery amplification is classified as being at a Level 2. Thus, this is considered advanced assistive automation rather than existing as an autonomous capacity. Meanwhile, in ready comparison, suppose that a competing vendor has an e-Discovery tool that is rated as a Level 3. All in all, one can readily construe that the Level 3 product has a superior level of an autonomous facility than the Level 2 offering. Thus, the use of this pragmatic scale enables a kind of above-board playing field and readily facilitates head-to-head comparison.

This same benefit can be realized in the legal research sphere too.

Suppose a legal scholar criticizes that AI legal reasoning algorithms are weak at identifying suitable sentencing recommendations. That might be a valid concern, though this could be based on studying say Level 1 such systems and therefore provides only a narrow perspective.

Other researchers might inadvertently misconstrue the result and assume that all AI-based legal reasoning systems are equally deficient, when in fact, it could be that Level 2 and Level 3 systems are more robust and have overcome the identified weakness. Researchers would be able to utilize the scale as part of their own legal research efforts, including applying the scale to other research results for the uncovering of hidden assumptions.

All told, a measuring scale of this nature has applicability to both the day-to-day world of business and the law, plus likewise applicability to legal scholarship.

Furthermore, this scale for AI legal reasoning serves as a wake-up call or catalyst for engaging in a timely and vital dialogue about how to best seek to rate or assess the emerging plethora of AI-enabled legal applications. Businesses that are gradually and inevitably going to be adopting these systems will need a convenient and apt means to compare and contrast competing products. Academics also are in need of a robust method for assessing how far along the advances in AI legal reasoning capacities have progressed.

Management scholar Peter Drucker had opined that you cannot suitably manage that which you are not measuring. For those in business law, having a set of autonomous levels pertaining to legal reasoning can provide a substantive benefit toward winnowing the LegalTech wheat from the chaff.

Note: *For supplemental materials depicting the aspects discussed in this chapter, refer to Appendix B, which contains various augmented diagrams, charts, and additional related facets of relevanc*

APPENDIX A
TEACHING WITH THIS MATERIAL
AND BIBLIOGRAPHY

The essays in this book can readily be used as a reading supplemental to augment traditional textbook-oriented content, particularly used in a class on AI or a class about the law.

Courses where this material is most likely applicable encompass classes at a college or university level.

Here are some typical settings that might apply:

o   <u>Computer Science</u>. Classes studying AI, or possibly a CS social impacts class, etc.

o   <u>Law</u>. Law classes exploring technology and its adoption for legal uses.

o   <u>Sociology</u>. Sociology classes on the adoption and advancement of technology.

Specialized classes at the undergraduate and graduate level can also make use of this material.

For each chapter, consider whether you think the chapter provides material relevant to your course topic.

There are plenty of opportunities to get the students thinking about the topics and encourage them to decide whether they agree or disagree with the points offered and positions taken.

I would also encourage you to have the students do additional research beyond the chapter material presented (I provide next some suggested assignments that they can do).

RESEARCH ASSIGNMENTS ON THESE TOPICS

Your students can find research and background material on these topics, doing so in various tech journals, law journals, and other related publications.

Here are some suggestions for homework or projects that you could assign to students:

a) <u>Assignment for foundational AI research topics</u>: Research and prepare a paper and a presentation on a specific aspect of AI, such as Machine Learning, ANN, etc. The paper should cite at least 3 reputable sources. Compare and contrast to what has been stated in the chosen chapter.

b) <u>Assignment for Law topics</u>: Research and prepare a paper covering Law aspects via at least 3 reputable sources and analyze the characterizations. Compare and contrast to what has been stated in the chosen chapter.

c) <u>Assignment for a Business topic</u>: Research and prepare a paper and a presentation on businesses and advanced technology regarding AI and Law. What is trending, and why? Make sure to cite at least 3 reputable sources. Compare and contrast to the depictions herein.

d) <u>Assignment to do a Startup:</u> Have the students prepare a paper or business plan about how they might start up a business in this realm. They could also be asked to present their business plan and should also have a prepared presentation deck to coincide with it.

You can certainly adjust the aforementioned assignments to fit your particular needs and class structure.

You'll notice that I usually suggest that (at least) 3 reputable cited sources be utilized for the paper writing-based assignments.

I usually steer students toward "reputable" publications, since otherwise, they will cite some less reliable sources that have little or no credentials, other than that they happened to appear online was easy to retrieve. You can, of course, define "reputable" in whatever way you prefer, for example, some faculty think Wikipedia is not reputable while others believe it is reputable and allow students to cite it.

The reason that I usually ask for at least 3 citations is that if the student only relies upon one or two citations, they usually settle on whatever they happened to find the fastest. By requiring 3 (or more) citations, it usually seems to inspire them to explore more extensively and likely end-up finding five or more sources, and then whittling it down to 3 if so needed.

I have not specified the length of their papers and leave that to you to tell the students what you prefer.

For each of those assignments, you could end up with a short one to two-pager or you could do a dissertation length in-depth paper. Base the length on whatever best fits for your class, and likewise the credit amount of the assignment within the context of the other grading metrics you'll be using for the class.

I usually try to get students to present their work, in addition to doing the writing. This is a helpful practice for what they will do in the business world. Most of the time, they will be required to prepare an analysis and present it. If you don't have the class time or inclination to have the students present their papers, then you can presumably omit the aspect of them putting together presentations.

GUIDE TO USING THE CHAPTERS

For each of the chapters, I provide the next some various ways to use the chapter contents.

You can assign the below tasks as individual homework assignments, or the tasks can be used for team projects. You can easily layout a series of assignments, such as indicating that the students are to do item "a" below for say Chapter 1, then "b" for the next chapter of the book, and so on.

a) What is the main point of the chapter and describe in your own words the significance of the topic.

b) Identify at least two aspects in the chapter that you agree with and support your concurrence by providing at least one other outside researched item as support; make sure to explain your basis for agreeing with the aspects.

c) Identify at least two aspects in the chapter that you disagree with and support your disagreement by providing at least one other outside researched item as support; make sure to explain your basis for disagreeing with the aspects.

d) Find an aspect that was not covered extensively in the chapter, doing so by conducting outside research, and then offer an expanded indication about how that aspect ties into the chapter, along with the added significance it brings to the topic.

e) Interview a specialist in the industry about the topic of the chapter, collect from them their thoughts and opinions, and readdress the chapter by citing your source and how they compared and contrasted to the material,

f) Interview a relevant professor or researcher in a college or university setting about the topic of the chapter, collect from them their thoughts and opinions, and readdress the chapter by citing your source and how they compared and contrasted to the material,

g) Try to update a chapter by finding out the latest on the topic and ascertain whether the issue or topic has now been solved or whether it is still being addressed, explain what you come up with.

The above are all ways in which you can get the students of your class involved in considering the material of a given chapter. You could mix things up by having one of those above assignments per each week, covering the chapters over the course of the semester or quarter.

SUGGESTED REFERENCES TO EXPLORE

To help get your students started in finding relevant and important papers on the topic of AI and the law, I provide next a handy bibliography that can be utilized.

You could also assign the students to each (or in teams) read an assigned reference from the list, and then have them provide either a written summary and review or do so as part of a classroom presentation.

BIBLIOGRAPHIC REFERENCES

1. Aleven, Vincent (1997). "Teaching Case-Based Argumentation Through a Model and Examples," Ph.D. Dissertation, University of Pittsburgh.

2. Aleven, Vincent (2003). "Using Background Knowledge in Case-Based Legal Reasoning: A Computational Model and an Intelligent Learning Environment," Artificial Intelligence.

3. Amgoud, Leila (2012). "Five Weaknesses of ASPIC+," Volume 299, Communications in Computer and Information Science (CCIS).

4. Antonious, Grigoris, and George Baryannis, Sotiris Batsakis, Guido Governatori, Livio Robaldo, Givoanni Siragusa, Ilias Tachmazidis (2018). "Legal Reasoning and Big Data: Opportunities and Challenges," August 2018, MIREL Workshop on Mining and Reasoning Legal Texts.

5. Ashley, Kevin (1991). "Reasoning with Cases and Hypotheticals in HYPO," Volume 34, International Journal of Man-Machine Studies.

6. Ashley, Kevin, and Karl Branting, Howard Margolis, and Cass Sunstein (2001). "Legal Reasoning and Artificial Intelligence: How Computers 'Think' Like Lawyers," Symposium: Legal Reasoning and Artificial Intelligence, University of Chicago Law School Roundtable.

7. Baker, Jamie (2018). "A Legal Research Odyssey: Artificial Intelligence as Disrupter," Law Library Journal.

8. Batsakis, Sotiris, and George Baryannis, Guido Governatori, Illias Tachmazidis, Grigoris Antoniou (2018). "Legal Representation and Reasoning in Practice: A Critical Comparison," Volume 313, Legal Knowledge and Information Systems.

9. Bench-Capon, Trevor (2004). "AGATHA: Automation of the Construction of Theories in Case Law Domains," January 2004, Legal Knowledge and Information Systems Jurix 2004, Amsterdam.

10. Bench-Capon, Trevor (2012). "Representing Popov v Hayashi with Dimensions and Factors," March 2012, Artificial Intelligence and Law.

11. Bench-Capon, Trevor, and Givoanni Sartor (2003). "A Model of Legal Reasoning with Cases Incorporating Theories and Values," November 2013, Artificial Intelligence.

12. Breuker, Joost (1996). "A Functional Ontology of Law," October 1996, ResearchGate.

13. Bruninghaus, Stefanie, and Kevin Ashley (2003). "Combining Case-Based and Model-Based Reasoning for Predicting the Outcome of Legal Cases," June 2003, ICCBR'03: Proceedings of the 5th International Conference on Case-based reasoning: Research and Development.

14. Buchanan, Bruce, and Thomas Headrick (1970). "Some Speculation about Artificial Intelligence and Legal Reasoning," Volume 23, Stanford Law Review.

15. Chagal-Feferkorn, Karni (2019). "Am I An Algorithm or a Product: When Products Liability Should Apply to Algorithmic Decision-Makers," Stanford Law & Policy Review.

16. Douglas, William (1948). "The Dissent: A Safeguard of Democracy," Volume 32, Journal of the American Judicature Society.

17. Dung, P, and R. Kowalski, F. Toni (2006). "Dialectic Proof Procedures for Assumption-Based Admissible Argumentation," Artificial Intelligence.

18. Eliot, Lance (2020). AI And Legal Reasoning Essentials. LBE Press Publishing.

19. Eliot, Lance (2020). Artificial Intelligence and LegalTech Essentials. LBE Press Publishing.

20. Eliot, Lance (2020). Decisive Essays on AI and Law. LBE Press Publishing.

21. Eliot, Lance (2020). Incisive Research on AI and Law. LBE Press Publishing.

22. Eliot, Lance (2020). Ingenious Essays on AI and Law. LBE Press Publishing.

23. Eliot, Lance (2020). "FutureLaw 2020 Showcases How Tech is Transforming The Law, Including the Impacts of AI," April 16, 2020, Forbes.

24. Erdem, Esra, and Michael Gelfond, Nicola Leone (2016). "Applications of Answer Set Programming," AI Magazine.

25. Gardner, Anne (1987). Artificial Intelligence and Legal Reasoning. MIT Press.

26. Genesereth, Michael (2009). "Computational Law: The Cop in the Backseat," Stanford Center for Legal Informatics, Stanford University.

27. Ghosh, Mirna (2019). "Automation of Legal Reasoning and Decision Based on Ontologies," Normandie Universite.

28. Grabmair, Matthias (2017). "Predicting Trade Secret Case Outcomes using Argument Schemes and Learned Quantitative Value Effect Tradeoffs," IJCAI June 12, 2017, London, United Kingdom.

29. Hage, Jaap (1996). "A Theory of Legal Reasoning and a Logic to Match," Volume 4, Artificial Intelligence and Law.

30. Hage, Jaap (2000). "Dialectical Models in Artificial Intelligence and Law," Artificial Intelligence and Law.

31. Hage, Japp, and Ronald Leenes, Arno Lodder (1993). "Hard Cases: A Procedural Approach," Artificial Intelligence and Law.

32. Hobbes, Thomas (1651). The Matter, Form, and Power of a Common-Wealth Ecclesiasticall and Civil.

33. Holmes, Oliver (1897). "The Path of the Law," Volume 10, Harvard Law Review.

34. Katz, Daniel, and Michael Bommarito, Josh Blackman (2017). "A General Approach for Predicting the Behavior of the Supreme Court of the United States," April 12, 2017, PLOS ONE.

35. Kowalski, Robert, and Francesca Toni (1996). "Abstract Argumentation," AI-Law96.

36. Laswell, Harold (1955). "Current Studies of the Decision Process: Automation Creativity," Volume 8, Western Political Quarterly.

37. Libal, Tomer, and Alexander Steen (2019). "The NAI Suite: Drafting and Reasoning over Legal Texts," October 15, 2019, arXiv.

38. Lipton, Zachary (2017). "The Mythos of Model Interpretability," March 6, 2017, arXiv.

39. Martin, Andrew, and Kevin Quinn, Theodore Ruger, Pauline Kim (2004). "Competing Approaches to Predicting Supreme Court Decision Making," December 2014, Symposium on Forecasting U.S. Supreme Court Decisions.

40. McCarty, Thorne (1977). "Reflections on TAXMAN: An Experiment in Artificial Intelligence and Legal Reasoning," January 1977, Harvard Law Review.

41. Modgil, Sanjay, and Henry Prakken (2013). "The ASPIC+ Framework for Structured Argumentation: A Tutorial," December 16, 2013, Argument & Computation.

42. Mowbray, Andrew, and Philip Chung, Graham Greenleaf (2019). "Utilising AI in the Legal Assistance Sector," LegalAIIA Workshop, ICAIL, June 17, 2019, Montreal, Canada.

43. Parasuraman, Raja, and Thomas Sheridan, Christopher Wickens (2000). "A Model for Types and Levels of Human Interaction with Automation," May 2000, IEEE Transactions on Systems, Man, and Cybernetics.

44. Popple, James (1993). "SHYSTER: A Pragmatic Legal Expert System," Ph.D. Dissertation, Australian National University.

45. Prakken, Henry, and Giovanni Sartor (2015). "Law and Logic: A Review from an Argumentation Perspective," Volume 227, Artificial Intelligence.

46. Rissland, Edwina (1988). Artificial Intelligence and Legal Reasoning: A Discussion of the Field and Gardner's Book," Volume 9, AI Magazine.

47. Rissland, Edwina (1990). "Artificial Intelligence and Law: Stepping Stones to a Model of Legal Reasoning," Yale Law Journal.

48. Searle, John (1980). "Minds, Brains, and Programs," Volume 3, Behavioral and Brain Sciences.

49. Sunstein, Cass (2001). "Of Artificial Intelligence and Legal Reasoning," University of Chicago Law School, Public Law and Legal Theory Working Papers.

50. Sunstein, Cass, and Kevin Ashley, Karl Branting, Howard Margolis (2001). "Legal Reasoning and Artificial Intelligence: How Computers 'Think' Like Lawyers," Symposium: Legal Reasoning and Artificial Intelligence, University of Chicago Law School Roundtable.

51. Surden, Harry (2014). "Machine Learning and Law," Washington Law Review.

52. Surden, Harry (2019). "Artificial Intelligence and Law: An Overview," Summer 2019, Georgia State University Law Review.

53. Valente, Andre, and Joost Breuker (1996). "A Functional Ontology of Law," Artificial Intelligence and Law.

54. Waltl, Bernhard, and Roland Vogl (2018). "Explainable Artificial Intelligence: The New Frontier in Legal Informatics," February 2018, Jusletter IT 22, Stanford Center for Legal Informatics, Stanford University.

55. Wittgenstein, Ludwig (1953). Philosophical Investigations. Blackwell Publishing.

APPENDIX B
SUPPLEMENTAL
FIGURES AND CHARTS

For the convenience of viewing, supplemental figures and charts related to the topics discussed are shown on the next pages

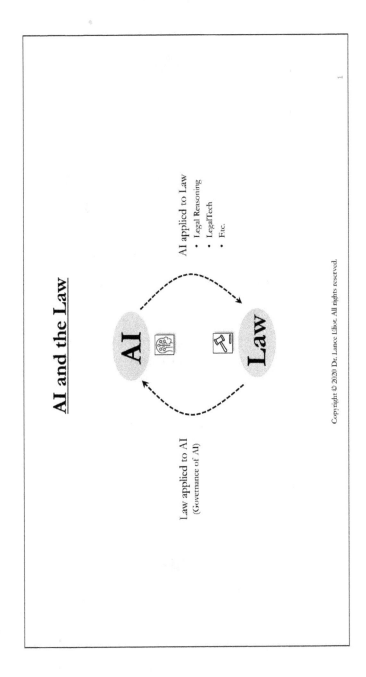

Figure 1

AI & Law: Levels of Autonomy For AI Legal Reasoning (AILR)

V1.3

Level	Descriptor	Examples	Automation	Status
0	No Automation	Manual, paper-based (no automation)	None	De Facto - In Use
1	Simple Assistance Automation	Word Processing, XLS, online legal docs., etc.	Legal Assist	Widely In Use
2	Advanced Assistance Automation	Query-style NLP, ML for case prediction, etc.	Legal Assist	Some In Use
3	Semi-Autonomous Automation	KBS & ML/DL for legal reasoning & analysis, etc.	Legal Assist	Primarily Prototypes & Research Based
4	AILR Domain Autonomous	Versed only in a specific legal domain	Legal Advisor (law fluent)	None As Yet
5	AILR Fully Autonomous	Versatile within and across all legal domains	Legal Advisor (law fluent)	None As Yet
6	AILR Superhuman Autonomous	Exceeds human-based legal reasoning	Supra Legal Advisor	Indeterminate

Figure 1: AI & Law - Autonomous Levels by Rows

Source Author: Dr. Lance B. Eliot

Figure 2

AI & Law: Levels of Autonomy For AI Legal Reasoning (AILR)

	Level 0	Level 1	Level 2	Level 3	Level 4	Level 5	Level 6
Descriptor	No Automation	Simple Assistance Automation	Advanced Assistance Automation	Semi-Autonomous Automation	AILR Domain Autonomous	AILR Fully Autonomous	AILR Superhuman Autonomous
Examples	Manual, paper-based (no automation)	Word Processing, XLS, online legal docs, etc.	Query-style NLP, ML for case prediction, etc.	KBS & ML/DL for legal reasoning & analysis, etc.	Versed only in a specific legal domain	Versatile within and across all legal domains	Exceeds human-based legal reasoning
Automation	None	Legal Assist	Legal Assist	Legal Assist	Legal Advisor (law fluent)	Legal Advisor (law fluent)	Supra Legal Advisor
Status	De Facto – In Use	Widely In Use	Some In Use	Primarily Prototypes & Research-based	None As Yet	None As Yet	Indeterminate

v1.3

Source Author: Dr. Lance B. Eliot

Figure 2: AI & Law - Autonomous Levels by Columns

Figure 3

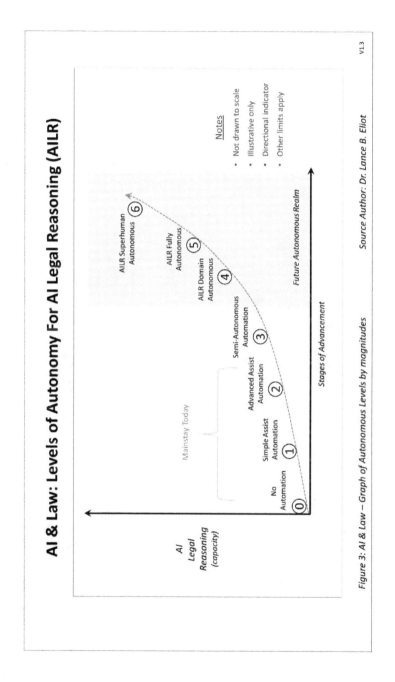

Figure 4

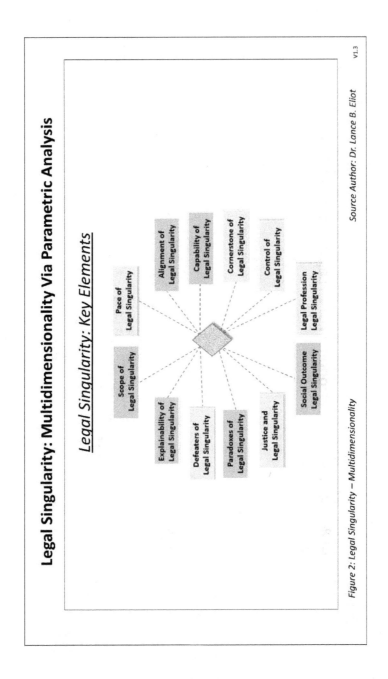

Figure 5

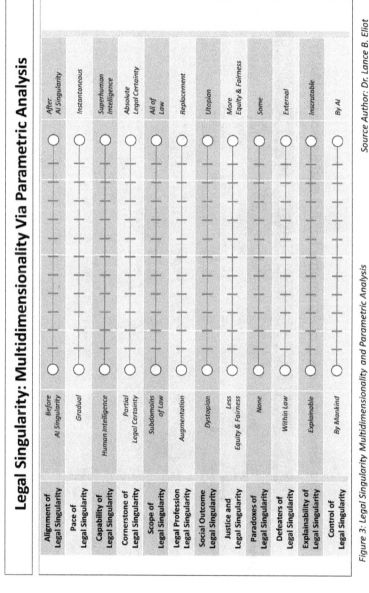

Legal Singularity: Multidimensionality Via Parametric Analysis

	Before AI Singularity					After AI Singularity
Alignment of **Legal Singularity**						
Pace of **Legal Singularity**	Gradual					Instantaneous
Capability of **Legal Singularity**	Human Intelligence					Superhuman Intelligence
Cornerstone of **Legal Singularity**	Partial Legal Certainty					Absolute Legal Certainty
Scope of **Legal Singularity**	Subdomains of Law					All of Law
Legal Profession **Legal Singularity**	Augmentation					Replacement
Social Outcome **Legal Singularity**	Dystopian					Utopian
Justice and **Legal Singularity**	Less Equity & Fairness					More Equity & Fairness
Paradoxes of **Legal Singularity**	None					Some
Defeaters of **Legal Singularity**	Within Law					External
Explainability of **Legal Singularity**	Explainable					Inscrutable
Control of **Legal Singularity**	By Mankind					By AI

Source Author: Dr. Lance B. Eliot

Figure 3: Legal Singularity Multidimensionality and Parametric Analysis

Figure 6

Legal Micro-Directives: Levels of Autonomy For AI Legal Reasoning (AILR)

	Level 0	Level 1	Level 2	Level 3	Level 4	Level 5	Level 6
Descriptor	No Automation	Simple Assistance Automation	Advanced Assistance Automation	Semi-Autonomous Automation	AILR Domain Autonomous	AILR Fully Autonomous	AILR Superhuman Autonomous
Examples	Manual, paper-based (no automation)	Word Processing, XLS, online legal docs, etc.	Query-style NLP, ML for case prediction, etc.	KBS & ML/DL for legal reasoning & analysis, etc.	Versed only in a specific legal domain	Versatile within and across all legal domains	Exceeds human-based legal reasoning
Automation	None	Legal Assist	Legal Assist	Legal Assist	Legal Advisor (law fluent)	Legal Advisor (law fluent)	Supra Legal Advisor
Status	De Facto – In Use	Widely In Use	Some In Use	Primarily Prototypes & Research-based	None As Yet	None As Yet	Indeterminate
AI-Enabled Legal Micro-Directives	*n/a*	*Impractical*	*Incubatory*	*Infancy*	*Narrow*	*Wide*	*Consummate*

v1.3

Figure 1: Legal Micro-Directives - Autonomous Levels of AILR by Columns   *Source Author: Dr. Lance B. Eliot*

Figure 7

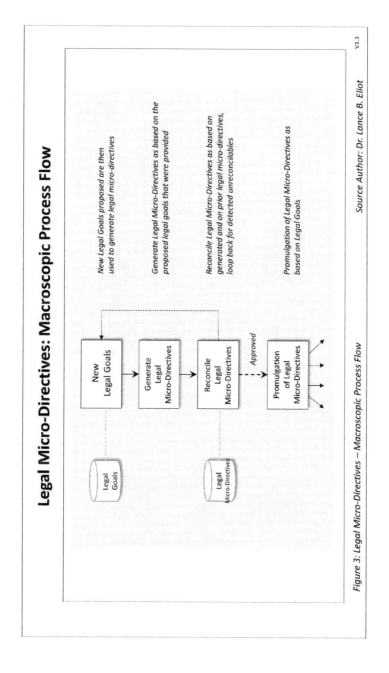

Figure 8

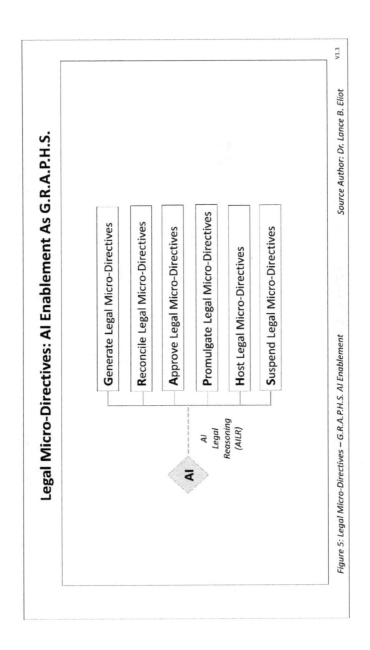

Figure 9

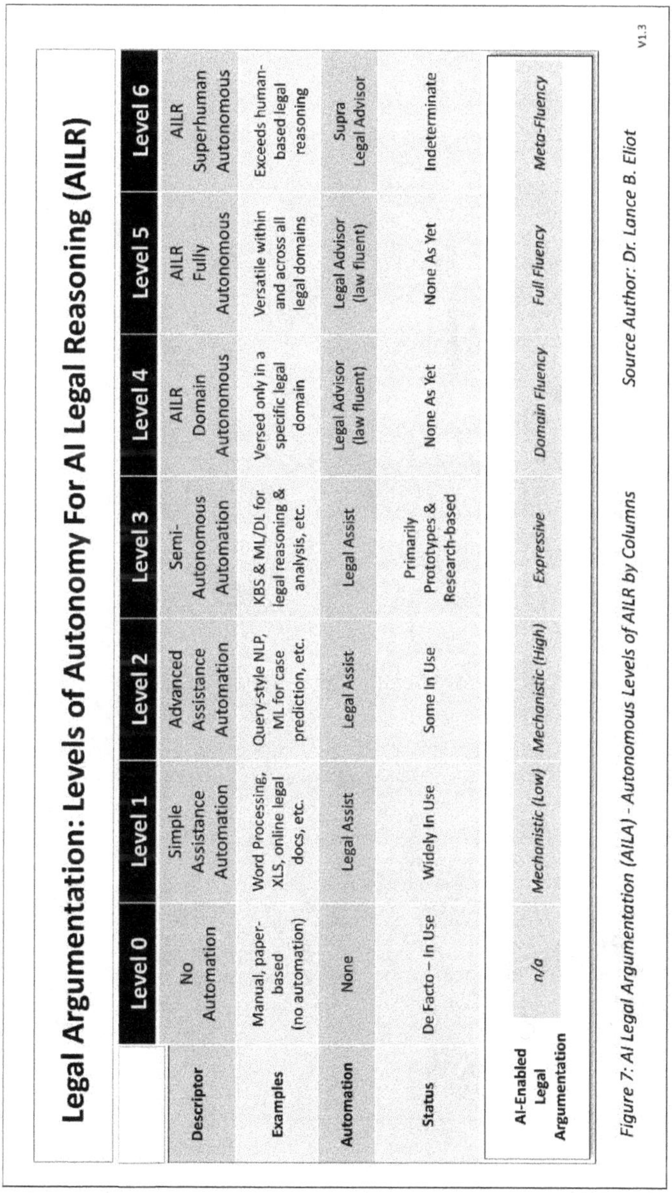

Legal Argumentation: Levels of Autonomy For AI Legal Reasoning (AILR)

	Level 0	Level 1	Level 2	Level 3	Level 4	Level 5	Level 6
Descriptor	No Automation	Simple Assistance Automation	Advanced Assistance Automation	Semi-Autonomous Automation	AILR Domain Autonomous	AILR Fully Autonomous	AILR Superhuman Autonomous
Examples	Manual; paper-based (no automation)	Word Processing, XLS, online legal docs, etc.	Query-style NLP, ML for case prediction, etc.	KBS & ML/DL for legal reasoning & analysis, etc.	Versed only in a specific legal domain	Versatile within and across all legal domains	Exceeds human-based legal reasoning
Automation	None	Legal Assist	Legal Assist	Legal Assist	Legal Advisor (law fluent)	Legal Advisor (law fluent)	Supra Legal Advisor
Status	De Facto – In Use	Widely In Use	Some In Use	Primarily Prototypes & Research-based	None As Yet	None As Yet	Indeterminate
AI-Enabled Legal Argumentation	n/a	Mechanistic (Low)	Mechanistic (High)	Expressive	Domain Fluency	Full Fluency	Meta-Fluency

v1.3

Figure 7: AI Legal Argumentation (AILA) - Autonomous Levels of AILR by Columns   Source Author: Dr. Lance B. Eliot

Figure 10

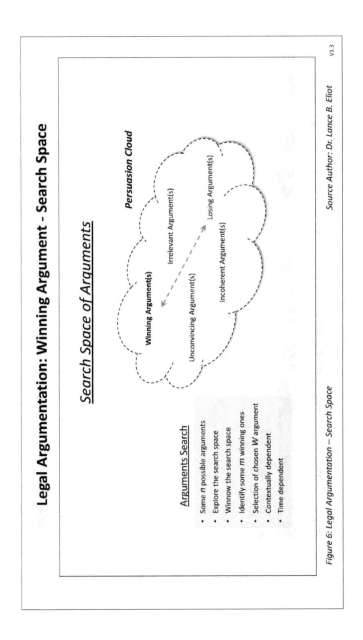

Figure 11

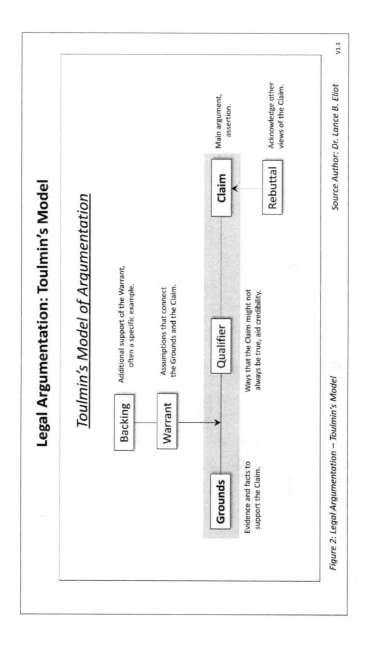

Figure 2: Legal Argumentation – Toulmin's Model

Figure 12

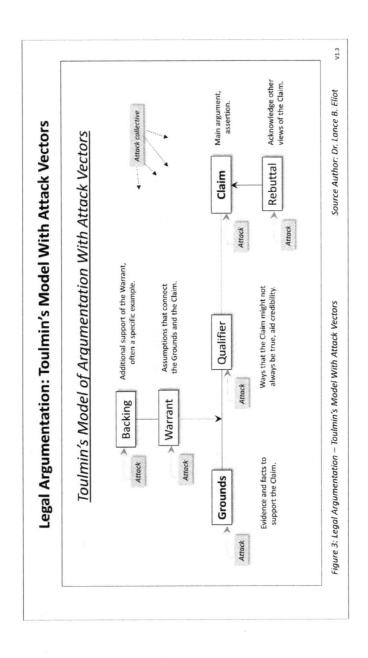

Figure 3: Legal Argumentation – Toulmin's Model With Attack Vectors

Figure 13

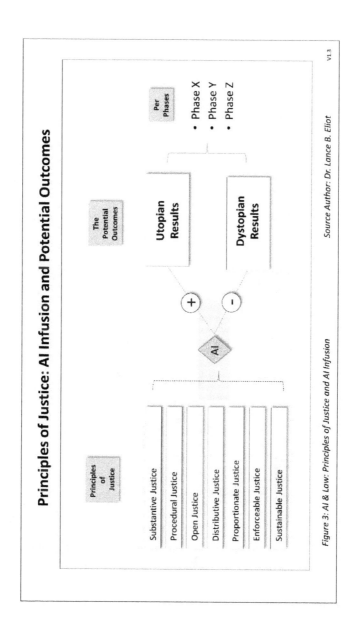

Figure 14

Principles of Justice and Autonomous Levels of AI Legal Reasoning (AILR)

Descriptor	Level 0	Level 1	Level 2	Level 3	Level 4	Level 5	Level 6
	No Automation	Simple Assistance Automation	Advanced Assistance Automation	Semi-Autonomous Automation	AILR Domain Autonomous	AILR Fully Autonomous	AILR Superhuman Autonomous
Substantive Justice	Traditional	Traditional	Traditional	Emerging	Phase X Impacts	Phase Y Impacts	Phase Z Impacts
Procedural Justice	Traditional	Traditional	Traditional	Emerging	Phase X Impacts	Phase Y Impacts	Phase Z Impacts
Open Justice	Traditional	Traditional	Traditional	Emerging	Phase X Impacts	Phase Y Impacts	Phase Z Impacts
Distributive Justice	Traditional	Traditional	Traditional	Emerging	Phase X Impacts	Phase Y Impacts	Phase Z Impacts
Proportionate Justice	Traditional	Traditional	Traditional	Emerging	Phase X Impacts	Phase Y Impacts	Phase Z Impacts
Enforceable Justice	Traditional	Traditional	Traditional	Emerging	Phase X Impacts	Phase Y Impacts	Phase Z Impacts
Sustainable Justice	Traditional	Traditional	Traditional	Emerging	Phase X Impacts	Phase Y Impacts	Phase Z Impacts

V1.3

Figure 1: AI & Law – Principles of Justice and LoA AILR by Columns

Source Author: Dr. Lance B. Eliot

Figure 15

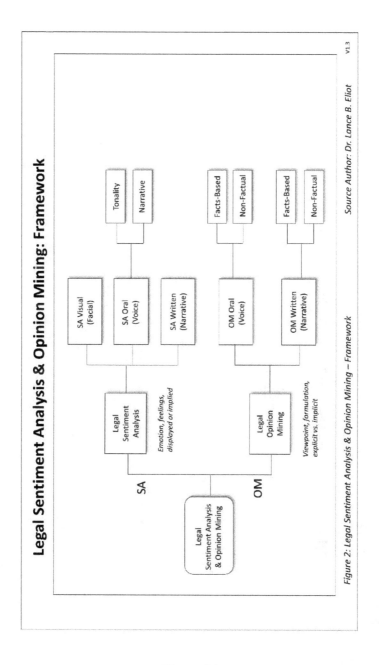

Figure 16

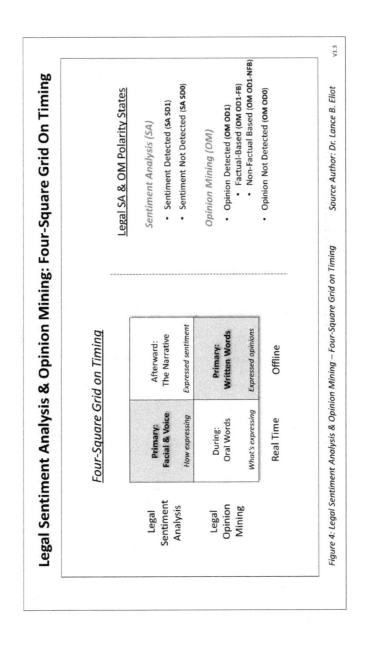

Figure 17

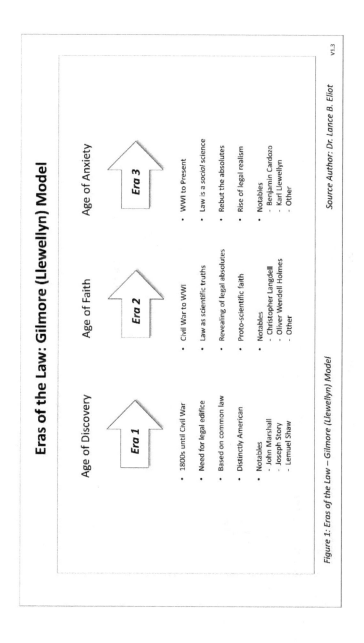

Figure 1: Eras of the Law – Gilmore (Llewellyn) Model

Figure 18

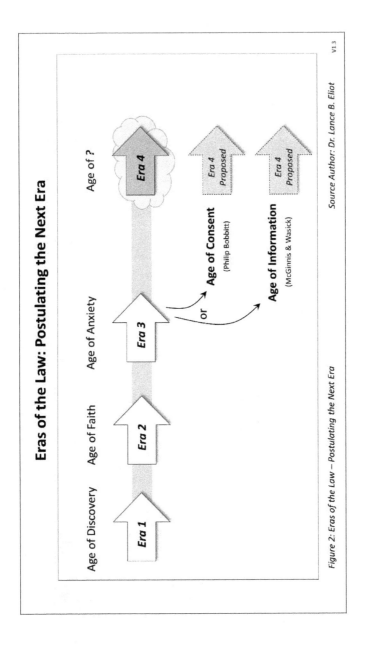

Figure 19

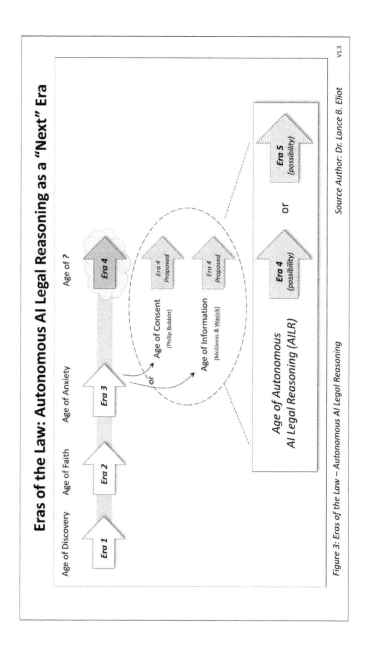

Figure 20

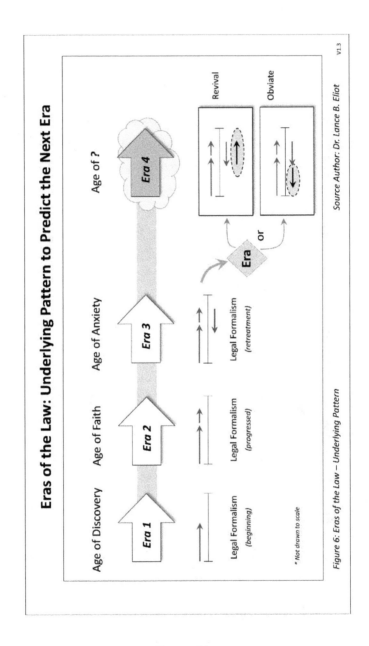

Figure 21

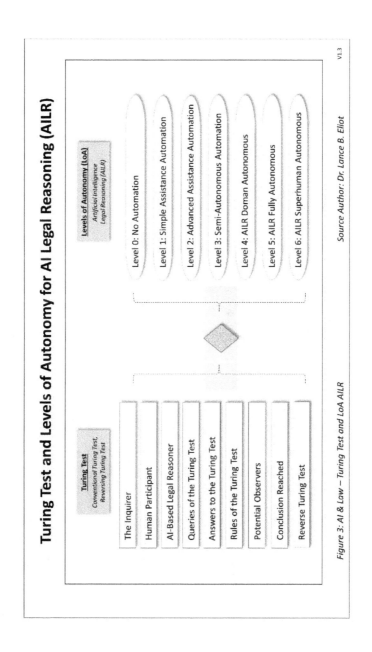

Figure 22

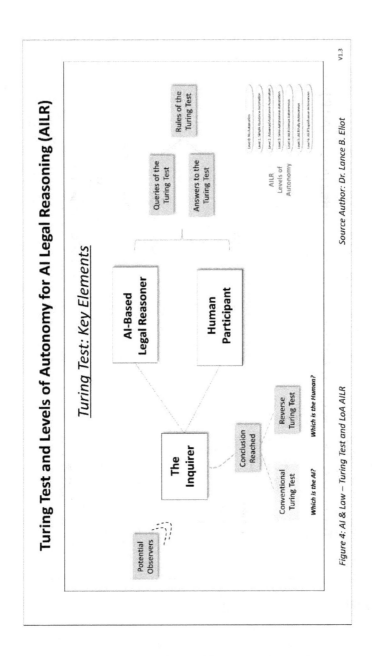

Figure 23

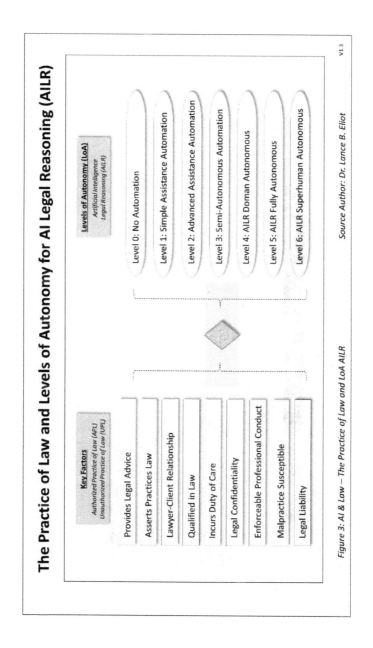

Figure 24

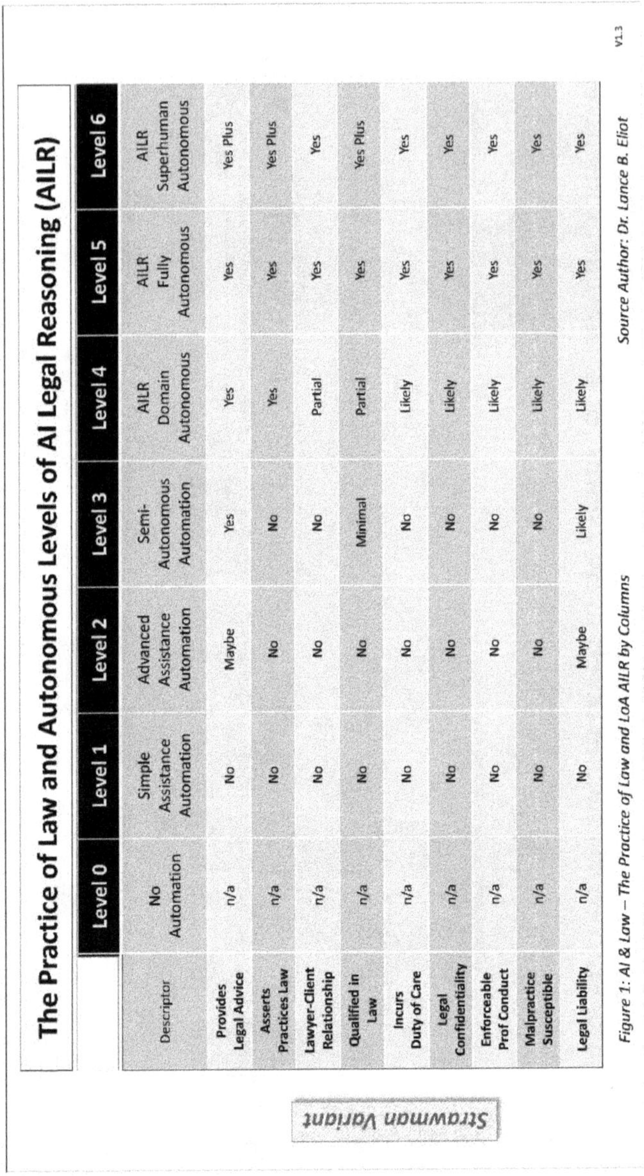

The Practice of Law and Autonomous Levels of AI Legal Reasoning (AILR)

Descriptor	Level 0 No Automation	Level 1 Simple Assistance Automation	Level 2 Advanced Assistance Automation	Level 3 Semi-Autonomous Automation	Level 4 AILR Domain Autonomous	Level 5 AILR Fully Autonomous	Level 6 AILR Superhuman Autonomous
Provides Legal Advice	n/a	No	Maybe	Yes	Yes	Yes	Yes Plus
Asserts Practices Law	n/a	No	No	No	Yes	Yes	Yes Plus
Lawyer-Client Relationship	n/a	No	No	No	Partial	Yes	Yes
Qualified in Law	n/a	No	No	Minimal	Partial	Yes	Yes Plus
Incurs Duty of Care	n/a	No	No	No	Likely	Yes	Yes
Legal Confidentiality	n/a	No	No	No	Likely	Yes	Yes
Enforceable Prof Conduct	n/a	No	No	No	Likely	Yes	Yes
Malpractice Susceptible	n/a	No	No	No	Likely	Yes	Yes
Legal Liability	n/a	No	Maybe	Likely	Likely	Yes	Yes

Strawman Variant

v1.3

Figure 1: AI & Law – The Practice of Law and LoA AILR by Columns

Source Author: Dr. Lance B. Eliot

Figure 25

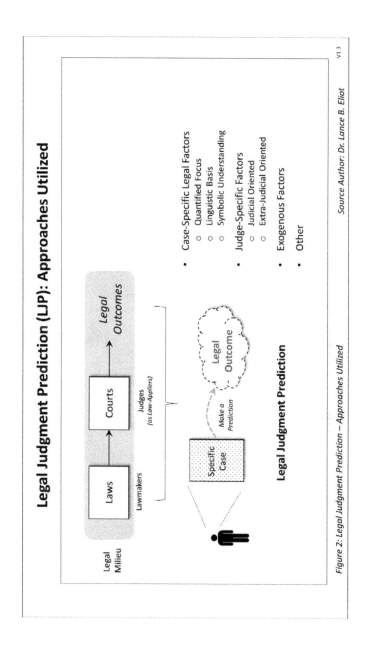

Figure 26

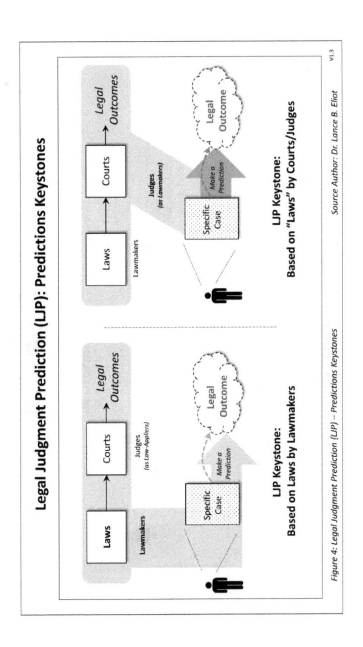

Figure 4: Legal Judgment Prediction (LJP) – Predictions Keystones

Figure 27

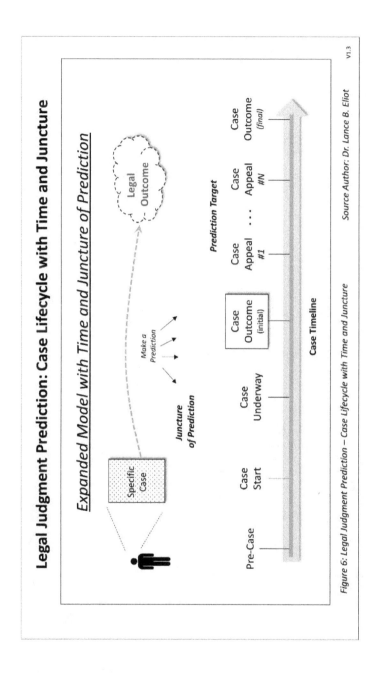

Figure 28

Dr. Lance B. Eliot

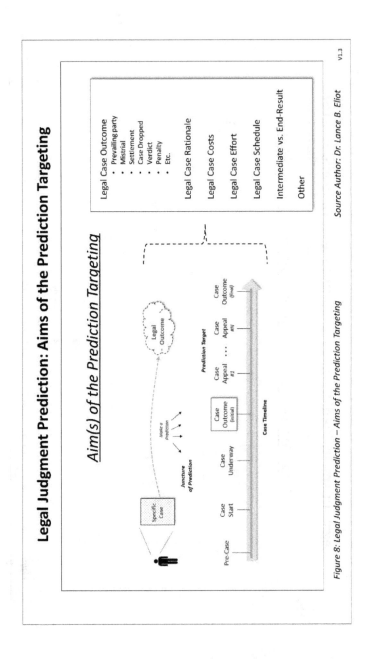

Figure 29

202

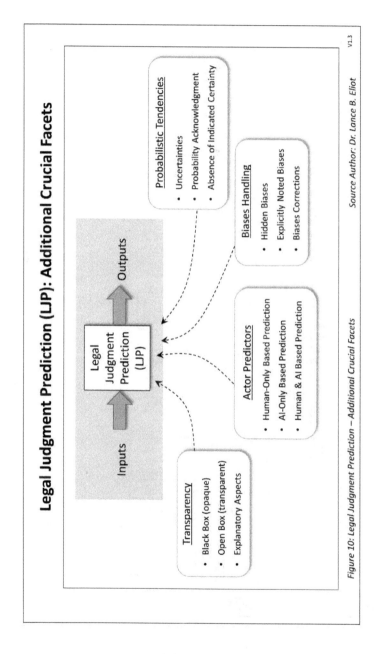

Figure 10: Legal Judgment Prediction – Additional Crucial Facets

Figure 30

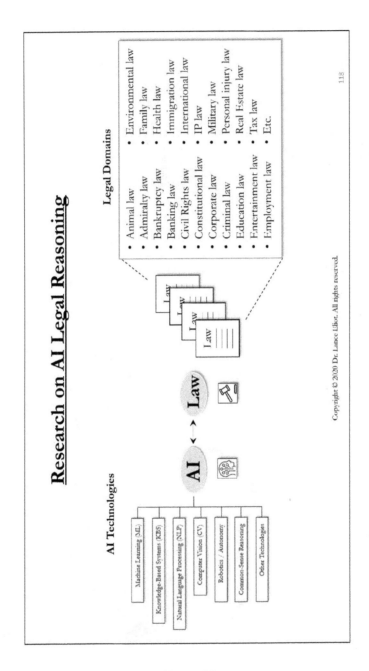

Figure 31

ABOUT THE AUTHOR

Dr. Lance B. Eliot, Ph.D., MBA is a globally recognized AI expert and thought leader, an invited Stanford Fellow at Stanford University, an experienced top executive and corporate leader, a successful entrepreneur, and a noted scholar on AI, including that his Forbes and AI Trends columns have amassed over 4 million views, his books on AI are ranked in the Top 10 of all-time AI books, his journal articles are widely cited, and he has developed and implemented numerous AI systems.

He currently serves as the Chief AI Scientist at Techbruim, Inc. and has over twenty years of industry experience including serving as a corporate officer in billion-dollar sized firms and was a partner in a major consulting firm. He is also a successful entrepreneur having founded, ran, and sold several high-tech related businesses.

Dr. Eliot previously hosted the popular radio show *Technotrends* that was also available on American Airlines flights via their in-flight audio program, he has made appearances on CNN, has been a frequent speaker at industry conferences, and his podcasts have been downloaded over 150,000 times.

A former professor at the University of Southern California (USC), he founded and led an innovative research lab on Artificial Intelligence. He also previously served on the faculty of the University of California Los Angeles (UCLA) and was a visiting professor at other major universities. He was elected to the International Board of the Society for Information Management (SIM), a prestigious association of over 3,000 high-tech executives worldwide.

He has performed extensive community service, including serving as Senior Science Adviser to the Congressional Vice-Chair of the Congressional Committee on Science & Technology. He has served on the Board of the OC Science & Engineering Fair (OCSEF), where he is also has been a Grand Sweepstakes judge, and likewise served as a judge for the Intel International SEF (ISEF). He served as the Vice-Chair of the Association for Computing Machinery (ACM) Chapter, a prestigious association of computer scientists. Dr. Eliot has been a shark tank judge for the USC Mark Stevens Center for Innovation on start-up pitch competitions and served as a mentor for several incubators and accelerators in Silicon Valley and in Silicon Beach.

Dr. Eliot holds a Ph.D. from USC, MBA, and Bachelor's in Computer Science, and earned the CDP, CCP, CSP, CDE, and CISA certifications

ADDENDUM

Thanks for reading this book and I hope you will continue your interest in the field of AI & Law

---

For my free podcasts about AI & Law:

https://ai-law.libsyn.com/website

Those podcasts are also available on Spotify, iTunes, etc.

For the latest on AI & Law see my website:

www.ai-law.legal

To follow me on Twitter:

https://twitter.com/LanceEliot

For my in-depth book on AI & Law:

AI And Legal Reasoning Essentials

www.amazon.com/gp/product/1734601655/